Cultivate Contentment

Using Ancient Wisdom to Thrive in Today's World

By Johanna Maheshvari Mosca, Ph.D.

Published by:
Sedona Spirit Yoga Publications
P.O. Box 278
Sedona, AZ 86339
928-282-9900
www.yogalife.net
peace@yogalife.net

Cover Art by Valerie Thang
www.bigstockphoto.com
Cover & Book Design by Karen Reider

Ordering Information:
To order additional copies directly from the author,
Johanna Maheshvari Mosca, Ph.D.,
please visit www.cultivatecontentment.com

ISBN 978-0-9679567-1-8

Printed in the U.S.A.

• Dedication •

This book is dedicated with love
to seven goddesses —

To my mother, Marge Mosca,
for giving me life and her big heart

To Maheshvari, for calling me forth
to be all I can be

To the three Goddesses
who helped deliver this baby:
Karen Reider, Carolyne Ruck, Pat Shapiro

To my sister, Carol Ann Wyberanec,
who is always there for me

And to that TV Goddess we cherish
as Patroness of Books

· Acknowledgement ·

I would like to acknowledge all of the
many wonderful people who gave me support
during this book writing process.
First, I would like to honor Patanjali
and all of the teachers and authors
who help expand our consciousness.
Thanks to the readers who took time to
give feedback and urged me to continue –
everyone from my hairdresser to my
neighbors, friends and even my realtor.
Special thanks to those who gave
glowing endorsements.
I am grateful for everyone's
enthusiastic response.

• Table of Contents •

Foreword by Terry Cole-Whittaker

Author's Preface

Part I, The Mindset for Contentment   1
   Chapter One — Applying These Principles   3
   Chapter Two — Silencing Your Monkey Mind   17
   Chapter Three — The Four D's for Transformation   29

Part II, Five Principles for Social Harmony   39
   Chapter One — Practice Compassion   41
   Chapter Two — Be Truthful   61
   Chapter Three — Respect What Belongs to Others   79
   Chapter Four — Manage Your Energy   91
   Chapter Five — Let Go of Possessiveness   101
   Summary — Creating Social Harmony   113

Part III, Principles for Personal Well-Being   115
   Chapter One — Keep it Clean   117
   Chapter Two — Cultivate Contentment   127
   Chapter Three — Develop Discipline   139
   Chapter Four — Study Yourself   151
   Chapter Five — Surrender to a Higher Power   167
   Summary – Achieving Personal Well-Being   181

Part IV, Essential Earth School Wisdom   183
   Enjoy Your Earth School Lessons   185

Footnotes   190

References   192

• Foreword •
by Terry Cole-Whittaker

When I wrote *What You Think of Me is None of My Business,* my intent was to encourage readers to let go of the need for approval from others and focus on the wealth within. I feel as if *Cultivate Contentment* might be called — *What I Think of Me is All of My Business.* In this age of quantum physics, it's becoming common knowledge that we manifest what we think, so our most important business is to mind our thoughts as well as our actions.

In bringing you this ancient wisdom, Johanna is opening the opportunity for you to look at your life vis-à-vis following ten important principles. She compassionately guides you to use tools for centering yourself, letting go of the past and designing what you want.

I have spent several years studying the ancient truths in the Vedic scriptures of India and know, personally, the strength of embracing this timeless knowledge. While many current texts contain the author's own opinions of what will make you happy, Johanna's book is revealing irrefutable, time-tested truths handed down by ancient sages.

As we are faced with the challenges of a troubled economy and mounting feelings of insecurity in the aftermath of 9/11, we need, more than ever, to rely on our inner strength and spiritual development. We must remember to abide by the core values of compassion and truthfulness. We need to consciously practice non-stealing, moderation and non-hoarding and limit what we consume.

We have to study ourselves and have the discipline to clean up our lives and develop daily contentment. We must surrender our ego's attachments and let go of trying to control the way life happens. We need to set up a system of "quality control" for our own behavior such as Johanna recommends in this book. Lastly, and primarily, we need to explore inner silence and dwell on our soul's connection to the Divine Source of energy that pervades all beings.

I am writing this foreword because I believe in Johanna and the way she has chosen to present this most important work. I believe that people need what she has to offer. And I look forward to the benefits that ripple out from this book as more and more readers practice this ancient wisdom to uplift today's world.

Imagine what a wonderful world it would be, how good we would all feel, if everyone practiced these principles. As you delve into the content of *Cultivate Contentment*, you will undoubtedly begin refining your life so as to become the best possible YOU. Actually, isn't that all we want — to be our best selves and be happy? My students know that whenever I see something wonderful in the world or in other people, I am fond of saying — "That's for me!" Well, all I can say about the prospect of having a world in which more of us practice these core values is a hearty — "That's for me!"

Terry Cole-Whittaker, D.D.
Adventures in Enlightenment Life Coach
Author of *Dare to Be Great* and *What You Think of Me is None of My Business*

· Author's Preface ·
by Johanna Mosca, Ph.D.

I have been writing to you for years it seems. But maybe I have just been writing to me. They say that the book writes the author. It's been about eight years in the writing and re-writing, to be exact. The message is so important to me that I wanted to get the words clear enough for them to mean something to you. And perhaps I needed the time to write and re-write what I was learning so that I could fully integrate it in my own life.

Yes, I have made all of the mistakes that people can make, and then some! They were good lessons disguised as mistakes. While I have taken every growth course I could find, it seems I have still lived my life by trial and error. Sometimes it feels as if I am starring in my own soap opera — "As I Live and Learn."

It's a bold step for me to launch a book called "Cultivate Contentment," as I am not a "Sally Sunshine" type of person. I am rather intense with a sun in Sagittarius, Aries rising and a moon in Virgo. This gives me a fiery personality and a dose of perfectionism to orchestrate. I always see what needs to be made better and strive for excellence. Yet, over the years, I have learned to consciously cultivate contentment as I ride through life's challenges and become less resistant to the bumps and potholes.

In these times of current economic uncertainty, we are all experiencing more stress and anxiety. It is as if America is like the phoenix rising from the ashes. First, we had that feeling of safety ripped out from under us by the terrorism of 9/11. Then we had the comfort of our never-ending credit and earning power threatened by economic uncertainty.

If there ever was a time, *this is the time* to focus on steadying ourselves from within and maintaining our own individual sense of core strength. While we are all aiming to practice the law of attraction, we need the foundation of a set of core values to accomplish our goals. We need to have our integrity intact to manifest what we want.

I have a solid core of values that guide me like a lighthouse through the dark or challenging moments. It is these values, gleaned from the wisdom of ancient Yoga sages, that I feel it is my legacy to share with you. Whenever I tell someone what I am writing about, the response is always an "ah-ha" of agreement that *we do need a return to values.*

The principles I am highlighting in this book are not at all new. It is the way that I am presenting them that is unique. I am offering them to you as a way to review your life up to this point in time, clear out the past with compassionate forgiveness, and start living these principles newly to cultivate greater contentment in your life moment by moment, day by day.

I am publishing this book because I am so sure that it will help people thrive. In some workshops I have attended in India, the teacher would start with a prayer that the content be nourishing and that peace prevail. Thus, *I turn these words over to you with a prayer that you will find them nourishing and they will contribute to greater peace in your life.*[1]

Read on, my friends, and let me know how much you enjoy cultivating contentment.

· Part I ·

The Mindset for Contentment

Chapter One

Applying These Principles

Maybe, like me, you are living your own soap opera "As I Live and Learn." I do know that whatever is going on for you, you are fine just the way you are, and I am writing this book to help you know that.

For whatever reason, being human somehow entails having the need to get better. If we all could get it, for once and for all, that we are perfect beings just the way we are — we would be content.

When we over-dramatize it, life is definitely a soap opera. The key to serenity is to minimize and dis-engage from the drama. Then it is possible to see life's lessons and be fully present to the learning experiences.

A common metaphor is that earth is a school and we are all students. Like it or not, we will be bombarded with lessons, big and small, some repeatedly until we finally learn them.

Following my own spiritual path, I have discovered a set of principles that help me remain clear and present to life — almost drama-free. In the succeeding chapters, I am offering them to you as recommended aids to contentment. From life experience, I can tell you that following these core principles makes life flow smoother and the Earth School lessons seem easier.

I always loved the newness of beginning a semester in school. Can you remember starting off a school year with a fresh notebook? Recall how nice it was to see the bright, blank white pages, offering a new beginning. I invite you to think of reading this book as giving yourself a new notebook in which the events of your life can unfold from this moment forward.

Consider yourself forgiven for anything you would like to erase from your past. Like a Fairy Godmother or the Good Witch of the West, I will wave my magic wand, absolving you of past regrets, and begin leading you on a journey of self-discovery.

You can take your blank notebook and make a fresh start by engaging in the guided processes of each chapter. You cannot do anything about the past. It is gone. The only thing you can do is release any emotional feelings you are still carrying from past soap opera dramas, learn their lessons and stay present in the new moment.

After discussing some tools for handling the mind, I will introduce ten ancient principles for social well-being and personal contentment. I believe that when we live according to these core principles of integrity, we align ourselves and our goals with the abundance of the universe.

These age-old principles have been around for many thousands of years. They brilliantly address two facets of life — social commitments and personal growth. It is often a juggling act to take care of numerous commitments to others — job, family, relationships — and still "make time" to take care of ourselves and pursue our personal interests. The first five principles are about creating harmony with others, and the second five are about fostering personal well-being.

Origin of the ten ancient principles

These ageless principles were part of a way of life taught by venerable Indian sages, first through the oral tradition and later recorded in ancient sacred texts. Over two thousand years ago, approximately three hundred years before Christ, a sage named

Patanjali is reported to have culled the wisdom of ancient Yoga philosophy and recorded it in a book now called the *Yoga Sutras of Patanjali.*

These ten principles and the great benefits of following them are among Patanjali's wise sayings for living a life free of suffering.[2] The sutras (threads of wisdom, aphorisms) speak of the pitfalls of being human and give guidelines to help all human beings combat problems.

There is little known about the author Patanjali, who is said to have been a doctor or a grammarian or both. Patanjali brilliantly collated this body of human knowledge into 195 succinct statements, organized in four books, systematically explaining: the nature of human consciousness; practices to develop freeing self-awareness; the extraordinary powers that can be reached; and the achievement of total freedom and serenity.

The *Yoga Sutras* of Patanjali did not originate with him but were the legacy of thousands of years of philosophy disseminated orally by numerous unnamed sages before him. Thus, as I take the liberty of adapting these ancient principles to modern life, I refer to this teaching as "the sages' wisdom."

Parts II and III of this book illustrate how you can use these ten principles to nurture yourself and your relationships. I invite you to explore how applying them with people and circumstances in your life can help you become more content.

Are you ready to live a life of heightened integrity and joyous satisfaction? From now on, you can excel at being you by using ten ancient principles to increase your own contentment and the well-being of all who come in contact with you.

Ten ancient principles to cultivate contentment

In Book II, sutras #29-45, of Patanjali's *Yoga Sutras*, he recommends ten codes of conduct as a foundation for living a contented life.[3] Each of the chapters in Parts II and III is devoted to one of the essential principles and the rewards of following it. As noted earlier, the first five are social codes for inter-personal harmony. Patanjali calls them "the mighty universal vows, not limited by place, time, circumstance or class."[4] He emphasizes that these values are universal and timeless.

Following these principles can help us enjoy rewarding relationships with the people with whom we live, work and play. Let's look at how they can help us avoid having our energy drained by those around us who might be consumed with drama and conflict. Applied to life in the twenty-first century, the social codes are:

1. Practice compassion   *Ahimsa*
2. Be truthful *Satya*
3. Respect what belongs to others *Asteya*
4. Manage your energy *Brahmacharya*
5. Let go of possessiveness *Aparigraha*

The second set of five principles can help us achieve personal fulfillment. These are internal observances focused on cultivating our well-being and highest self-development. They are guidelines for becoming fully present and at peace in each moment. Adapted to life today, the principles for self-mastery are:

1. Keep it clean *Saucha*
2. Cultivate contentment *Santosha*
3. Develop discipline *Tapas*
4. Study yourself *Svadhaya*
5. Surrender to a higher power *Ishvara Pranidhana*

The sages tell us that there are ongoing rewards for adhering to these essential life standards. Through the practice of these principles, we can develop greater awareness, discernment and clarity about the best choices to make. We can use the principles to access truth, inner knowing and strength. They can become signposts to help us make empowering decisions and lifelong commitments to achieve the highest good and the greatest peace.

The principles for social harmony and self-mastery are not commandments to adopt or rigid rules to follow. They are human values that have withstood the test of time in all cultures and all countries. The ten essential guides simply remind us to focus on the clarity and goodness we already possess inside our core consciousness.

When we practice these principles, we are able to respond to whatever life tosses at us with admirable performance, as if all the shots hit the sweet spots of our tennis racquets. When we violate them, things can tend to run amuck, and we may experience problems and drama. Following them helps us achieve greater success on both a personal and inter-personal level. We can use the principles as a foundation to rely on as we move through the lessons of Earth School, doing our best to honor ourselves and others.

Universal wisdom for people of all religions

I would like to dispel any erroneous notions you might have about the word "Yoga" and clarify its true meaning. The word Yoga means "to yoke" or "to harness." Yoga is defined as "union of the body, mind and spirit." While most often misconstrued as referring to only physical postures, Yoga is mainly about harnessing the true, core essence of the self. It is more about achieving inner peace than about "putting your foot in your ear."

These two sets of principles are the first two limbs or the foundation of Yoga. It is not necessary for you to know anything about Yoga or to do Yoga poses to reap the benefits of following these core principles. They contain kernels of universal wisdom for everyone.

The codes of conduct noted in *The Yoga Sutras* of Patanjali do *not* belong to any religion. While they do dovetail with Hindu and Buddhist beliefs, they complement the broad teachings of all religions. The principles foster the goals of every religion and of spirituality in general as they are designed to help human beings transcend life's challenges, live in harmony and become the best people possible.

What does contentment mean?

Cultivate Contentment adapts these ten ancient codes of conduct into modern practices to help you bring greater satisfaction and joy into your everyday life. What does it mean to be content? The ancient Yoga sages defined contentment as "unexcelled or supreme joy," noting that "there is nothing higher than satisfaction. It is complete in itself." Contentment is further defined as "delight with whatever fate may bring; evenness toward hardship and ease, as well as toward things one has obtained and those that are far from one's reach."[5]

What would it take for you to be content through life's ups and downs? What negative thoughts and behaviors would you have to give up? How can you keep yourself even and balanced amid your personal soap opera dramas and Earth School lessons? These are questions for you to explore while reading this book.

Usually, study in school requires mastering whatever it takes to meet the standards set by others. The purpose of our inquiry here is to have each of us develop — according to our own standards — into the best person we can be. In this Earth School teaching, the only standards to be met are the ones that we set up for ourselves.

Adapt familiar principles for new contentment

I invite you to adopt the ten principles as standards or guidelines to help you attain your most harmonious presence and greatest satisfaction with daily living — your own "contentment."

When your intention is to practice these principles, you are choosing the higher consciousness that is your natural birthright over all of the negative mental chatter that can come with being human. In the next chapter, we will look into distinguishing between your "higher consciousness" or inner awareness and your automatic voice or rambling "Monkey Mind." The choice is always yours — whether you want to enjoy full aliveness or fall back into the same old patterns.

At first glance, you might skim the principles and think — "I already know that!" The principles recommended here are not new. You probably learned them in kindergarten. However, if you take a closer look at situations in your everyday life, you will be amazed at how often you do *not* practice them. Never blame yourself.

What *Cultivate Contentment* offers that *is* new and original is the opportunity for you to use these timeless principles — combined with the law of attraction and the power of intention — to upgrade the quality of your daily life. This is your chance to review your life in a unique blame-free process, let go of what you would like to release and enrich your present circumstances. Now is the time to clear out the old, set new standards to live by and design the life you want. This book is a concrete step-by-step guide to help you look at your life through the lens of each principle, ask yourself specific questions, gain insights into what is most rewarding and set intentions from now on.

Three myths about life

There are many myths about being human that we all inherited from our ancestors. These myths are so strongly held in our culture that they weigh us down and darken our outlook. Let's examine the truth of three of these beliefs.

> **Myth 1:   You are not good enough and need to focus on getting better**

> *Truth:*   *See yourself as "perfect-and-developing" rather than as "needing-to-get-better"*

Do you think of yourself as a person who needs to get better? Just about everyone I know wants to get better. It's as if we are all born with an "I'm-not-good-enough" gene that we have to overcome. The "need-to-get-better" concept carries with it the belief that we do not fully accept ourselves exactly as we are.

I would like to suggest that you replace the "need-to-get-better" model with the "perfect-developing-being" model. This entails accepting yourself as "perfect" exactly as you are. However flawed and "imperfect" you might perceive yourself to be, <u>you are</u>

a perfect being whose true essence is unfolding. Instead of having harsh judgment about the lessons you are learning in Earth School, you can shift to appreciating them as steps toward excelling at being you.

Can you see yourself being perfect just the way you are in this very moment? Perhaps it would help to dismiss the notion of "perfect" as meaning "incapable of error" or "supremely flawless and ideal." Perfect means "accepted as is." It means that you are what you are and you are not what you are not. When you appreciate yourself the way you are and do not pretend to be what you are not, you are being authentic and perfect. This does not mean you do not have room for growth and advancement or that you should not strive for excellence.

You know that you are not static or flawed, though you have some tendencies you would like to shift. You are always in the process of expressing your energy in different ways. You may express cheerfulness or sadness, restlessness or laziness, interest or disinterest, silence or talkativeness. Your energy both reflects and affects your thoughts, feelings and emotions.

You undergo constant change in your energy vibration. It is important to view yourself as an energy being who is constantly changing vibration and who can choose to uplift that vibration at any time. The purpose of this book is to have you use these ten principles to make choices that uplift your thoughts, feelings and emotions to create a general attitude of contentment.

I invite you to see yourself as good enough now. If you are like most people, you probably are your own worst critic. As you go through your learning process, you might give yourself report card grades for every little subject in Earth School. You can choose to shift this perspective and see yourself as a perfectly "good enough" student who sometimes makes mistakes or poor choices as you go through your growth process.

Like everyone else, you have unwanted tendencies that sometimes sabotage your progress. At times you may get discouraged as you think you have moved three steps forward and two steps back. Still, you are a developing being, expanding into the fullness of your potential. As you become more aware, you will abandon things that no longer seem good for you.

Being authentic is being able to accept all of who you are — including your brightest light and your darkest secrets. As your soap opera unfolds, you do some things that work out well and others that you wish you could erase from the universe. Yet, all the while, you can remain authentic.

It is important to understand and accept your own "shadow" side. Tell the truth about who you are, including your undesirable tendencies and vulnerable feelings. Learn to recognize when they are present, shift your energy and move beyond them. When you do accept yourself fully, the patterns that no longer support your growth will diminish sooner or later.

It is beneficial to replace the deficiency model with a developmental paradigm. You are already good enough. You are perfect as-is, and you are expanding in consciousness as you grow and make new choices. Know that all of the choices you made in the past were necessary to bring you to this point of growth in your life, so even the ones that did not work out so well were good choices, too.

Myth 2: You have to work hard to overcome your shortcomings

Truth: You attract and increase whatever you focus your energy on

law of Attraction

The more attention you pay to constantly trying to change your shortcomings, the more energy you are expending to keep them alive and growing. It is common knowledge that "What you resist, persists." Since the universe does not hear the words "not" or "no," whatever you put a lot of energy into "not wanting" will be what you attract to yourself.

For instance, if a woman keeps saying "no more men like my ex-husband!" — the universe will not hear the word "no" and will keep sending her more men who are just like her ex-husband.

You must remember that in pushing anything away, you are giving it a lot of energy that will bring it back to you. Change can only happen when you are able to let go of resistance. All there is to do is to recognize what you would like to shift and allow it to be the way it is for now.

The theories of Quantum Physics teach that thought creates reality and that you will continue to manifest what you are thinking. Popular expressions of these theories appear in the teachings of the *Law of Attraction* spoken by Abraham through Esther Hicks, *The Secret* by Rhonda Byrne and numerous books and CD's by Drs. Gregg Braden, Deepak Chopra, Wayne Dyer and Eckhart Tolle as well as Louise L. Hay and others.[6]

You need to stay aware of where you are directing your attention. If you call for success and prosperity while engaged in thoughts of failure and loss, you will get more of what is occupying your unconscious vibration. To change any situation, you need to shift your thinking.

When you bewail your negative circumstances over and over, you are asking the universe to send more of the same because that is where you are putting your attention. For example, you might be lamenting that finances are low and sending out repeated messages of shortage of funds which — when the universe matches the vibration you are sending — keeps the situation the same. It is best to fully accept the unwanted circumstances for the time-being and put your attention on what you would like to manifest in the future.

If you are preoccupied with blame, guilt, regret or any sort of self-torment over the past, you are *not* open to see what's coming toward you in the present moment. The way to attract the solution is to dwell on the positive characteristics you are intending to achieve. Perhaps visualize having more clients or getting a raise or selling something for a huge profit. It would be much more beneficial to focus attention on income increasing. Repeating this kind of message sends the universe the idea that money is on its way — a much more positive vibration.

To attract the prosperity and joy that you aim to achieve, you need to constantly release negative thoughts and practices that block success. Only by accessing your higher consciousness can you attract the wonderful abundance you choose to manifest.

Myth 3: You have to suffer; it is unavoidable

Truth: You do have to experience some pain but you can avoid adding emotional misery called "suffering"

No one can avoid past suffering, but you can be aware of disturbing influences and refrain from giving them a lot of energy. You cannot avoid past anguish, but through heightened awareness, you can stop dwelling on it. While a certain amount of pain is inevitable in life, suffering entails adding greater emotional misery to the pain.

You may have heard stories of people with chronic illnesses remaining cheerful and benevolent throughout painful body breakdowns, and you may have seen the opposite in people who loudly lament and suffer over the slightest ailment. The sages see suffering as resisting what is. Once you accept what is, you can minimize its impact.

Know that suffering is a choice. You cannot control what happens to you in life. It's helpful to view life as having changes you might call "ups and downs." Sometimes you are at the top of your game and life is flowing with grace and ease, showering you with successes. At other times, as you experience the downside, you may have to endure losses such as money challenges, illness or car accidents.

All that you can control is the way you respond to whatever comes. Becoming emotionally devastated when unwanted circumstances occur is a choice. You can decide not to add heightened feelings of misery but to focus your energy on possible solutions and the many blessings you have in your life.

The more aware you become, the more you can refrain from engaging in negative thinking and, thereby, prevent future suffering. The more present and detached you are, the more you can anticipate and prevent what might tend to cause suffering.

In the *Yoga Sutras*, Patanjali states — "The pains which are yet to come can be and are to be avoided."[7] You can be more alert to look for the signs of static coming your way, such as unusual behavior from a relationship partner or extremely competitive behavior on the part of a colleague. As you detect these signals in advance, you can move more slowly and inquire into circumstances rather than be forced to react to them.

The more aware you are of the energies you perceive, the more able you are to handle potential challenges before they escalate into being giant problems. The more conscious you are of the choices you make and the practices you follow, the more foresight you will have to avoid suffering.

Actually, it is succumbing to the negative, automatic babbling of the "Monkey Mind" that creates suffering. The more you listen to the drama the mind adds, the worse you feel. When you focus on your inner strength, you are able to endure pain without adding suffering. Can you imagine making a decision not to suffer over anything from now on?

In upcoming chapters, you will have the opportunity to reflect on memories of life experiences that may have involved suffering. When you reflect on the journal questions provided, your automatic mind might want to have you re-run some past suffering. Do your best to forgive and let go of any negative incidents that may come up rather than use them to manufacture more misery. The purpose of reflecting is to clear yourself and to lighten up. When you allow yourself to bring something to the surface, just the act of bringing it to awareness is the beginning of dissolving it.

Keep it light

It is important to keep it light and maintain your sense of humor as you journey through the ups and downs of being enrolled in Earth School. As long as you know that you are a student and a developing being, you do not have to pretend to be perfect and strong all of the time. Perhaps you can turn your soap opera, "As I Live and Learn," into a romantic comedy.

You can see the humorous side of life and allow for margins of error as you go from lesson to lesson, learning some better than others, some faster, some perhaps "not yet." By lessons learned, I am not referring to harsh slaps on the wrist, but to the "Ah-ha's!" of life — the new realizations and expanded understandings. After all, the purpose of learning these lessons, or noticing where shift needs to happen, is to access the joy within.

Guided processes for each principle

Before applying the ten principles, it is important to first set a foundation for how to adapt them to everyday life. This section introduced the benefits of applying these ancient principles more fully in our lives. In the next chapter, we will look at how our minds work and how we can learn to bypass the automatic bombardment of superficial thoughts in order to access the deeper consciousness within. We will also explore using the Four D's, a unique four-step practice I developed for transforming any disturbing thoughts into desired outcomes.

And, finally, with a deeper understanding of how our minds work and some tools for manifesting our best selves, we will look at fully living each of the ten principles, starting with the first and paramount one, compassion. As we explore the principles for social harmony and personal growth, we will look at numerous examples of the benefits of applying each principle in daily life. You will be invited to ponder the principles, ask yourself some pertinent reflection questions, note your thoughts, appreciate what you notice and set intentions to achieve from now on.

Through non-judgmental, compassionate reflection, you can let go of any blocks to your energy flow. You can release and heal past issues. You can drop any "baggage" you may be carrying and free up your life. Best of all, you can access your inner knowing and peace. In doing so, you contribute that heightened well-being to your family, colleagues and everyone you meet.

To help you understand your thinking process, we will now distinguish between the thoughts that ramble through a superficial "Monkey Mind" and thoughts that emanate from a deeper conscious awareness.

Chapter Two

Silencing Your Monkey Mind

Before you look further into using the ten principles to enhance well-being, it is important to look at what kind of thinking you will use to apply them. Have you ever lay in bed at night, listening to your mind rattle on before you go to sleep? This stream-of-consciousness, incessant, babbling that goes on inside your head is often called the "Monkey Mind" in Yoga. You have to control the bombardment of automatic negative thoughts. It is the aim of Yoga to still the automatic mind so that you can access the deeper wisdom of the core consciousness within.

Several years ago, I camped atop Mt. Shasta and had many philosophical conversations with a Russian veterinarian, who had a wonderful way with words. He told me to forget about my "bill board" and focus on my "essence." Take a moment to draw those distinctions for yourself. What is your bill board, your website, the banners you use to present yourself to the world? Your job description, your titles, your roles, your personality, your education and all that you have accomplished are part of your bill board. We can call the bill board your ego, and it is the home of your Monkey Mind.

Then there is your essence, the YOU inside that has no credentials and just is. Your essence clamors for you to slow down and savor being alive. It is your conscious awareness that watches you do all of the accomplishing and encourages you to stop and enjoy the moment. Your essence is the quiet part of you that feels your connectedness with all of life. Your essence is a piece of the formless, all-being consciousness that embodies the whole universe.

The sages made similar distinctions between tangible form and matter found in nature and the formlessness of the pervasive universal consciousness. They call the bill board "Prakriti," a Sanskrit word for matter and form or the physical dimensions of man and nature. In contrast, they speak of the "Purusha" or all-being formless consciousness in which each of us shares a part, our inner core of conscious awareness.

Choosing higher consciousness over the Monkey Mind

You might recognize this "quiet within" as the peace you feel when you are absorbed in being in a magnificent scene in nature or humming along as you engage in a favorite hobby or even holding an infant in your arms. It is the place of intense inner peace and calm that everyone has inside. It is you being fully present to life without the distraction of your automatic mental banter.

There is a limitless consciousness within, buried beneath the chaotic chattering. Some might call it our soul essence, our core being or even our higher self. Each of us contains the universal energy that generates and connects all of life. We vibrate with the pulse of life. We are connected to all that happens in the universe and have the energy of the all-being consciousness within us. Our core consciousness is both our connection to the forces of the universe and a place of inner peace and innate knowledge.

It is as if there is one huge higher consciousness in the universe and each of us is a tiny piece of that vast consciousness. We are much like the drop is to the ocean or the grain of sand is to the beach or the stitch is to the tapestry. All we need to do is enter the stillness within and we can connect with that higher consciousness.

In *A New Earth*, Eckhart Tolle calls this inner state "the presence" and tells readers that "whenever they notice they have slipped back into a dysfunctional state, they are able to choose to step out of identification with thinking and emotion and enter the state of presence."[8] Unfortunately, our incessant mental chatter often keeps us from being fully present and is so prevalent that many of us identify with its content instead of dismissing it.

The wisdom of the first four of Patanjali's *Yoga Sutras* captures this distinction. They say that the way to achieve peace is to settle the mind into silence. "When the mind has settled, we are established in our essential nature, which is unbounded consciousness," but our "essential nature is usually overshadowed by the activity of the mind."[9]

In other words, when you are able to quiet the Monkey Mind, you can access your true inner splendor. When you are unable to quiet the Monkey Mind, you identify with it and think that what it says is who you are. Rather than go through life identifying with the rambling chatter, you can learn to access the pure awareness at your core.

Your Monkey Mind

Surely you've heard the expression — "You are not your thoughts." The automatic, rambling Monkey Mind jumps all over the place. It invalidates, judges, blames, criticizes and spews an endless diatribe of opinions. The automatic mind is driven by the ego and its need for uniqueness, approval, control, security and separation. You can listen to it run rampant when you feel that someone in your family or at your job is being favored over you.

The Monkey Mind is obsessed with "Me, My, I, Mine." It is preoccupied with getting its needs and desires met. It's like the screaming, egotistical child who stamps his feet, wanting what he wants NOW as if he is the only person in the world. The ego-driven mind is the part of you that can feel withdrawn, misunderstood and resentful. It is constantly searching for something missing that is going to make it all better in the future.

Your Monkey Mind looks outside of itself for satisfaction, makes constant comparisons and is competitive. It reacts hastily without thinking and has scattered attention. It finds fault with your lot in the universe. It wants to be alone and tells you that it is *"You against them."*

When you have a vision of achieving something, the babbling mind is the voice that comes in with all of the reasons why you cannot succeed. Its motto is "not-good-enough." The Monkey Mind takes everything personally and is like Velcro for insults. It snowballs small forgivable oversights into major unforgettable incidents. It is definitely not your friend!

Your core essence

When you are able to silence the automatic chatter, you can access your true essence and inner knowing. This higher being is your profound self. It watches over you and makes the right choices despite the blaring Monkey Mind.

This is your limitless capacity to achieve whatever you dream possible. It's the "yes I can" part of you. It is the part of you that has patience and can bide time without reacting. Your pure awareness can witness life without judging. Your core consciousness can be happy for the prosperity of others and be grateful for your own share of abundance.

It is your higher self, the best you that enjoys participating and loves being with people. It feels a part of the community, likes to cooperate and appreciates the differences in individuals. It is guided by your inner spirit and its sense of oneness.

Your core essence knows that people are all connected to each other and are part of the oneness. Your higher consciousness can be captivated with childlike wonder while watching a butterfly or a bird in the present moment. It slows you down and makes you more aware of yourself in action, serving as the objective witness to all you experience.

Your true inner being accepts things the way they are and generously allows everything to be okay. Like Teflon, it allows negativity to slide away rather than holding on to it. This is your expanding consciousness and your connection to universal energy, whose motto is "it's all good."

You can choose

As you can see, the ego-driven mind is like a rather loud chorus drowning out the beautiful voice of the opera star that comes from within. It seems bent on keeping you obsessing about past hurts or fantasizing about the future. It does not let you be still and rest in the present moment. When you are focused in the present moment without the distractions of the automatic mind, you are able to see what works and what does not. You are one-hundred-percent present and respond fully to whatever is happening now.

Stop for a moment and think about it. Which one do you listen to most of the time — your Monkey Mind or your core essence? Look at the chart on the next page. It shows the contrasting properties of each way of thinking. Scan the list of features in both columns of the chart. Think about which ones describe your most frequent thoughts. If the answer is your Monkey Mind, what can you do to silence it?

Which do you spend more time focusing on?

Monkey Mind	Core Essence
▲ your ego	▲ your higher self
▲ outward-looking	▲ inward-looking
▲ seeks approval from others	▲ trusts in self-approval
▲ creates separation (me vs. them)	▲ sees connectedness, oneness
▲ competes	▲ cooperates
▲ likes conflict	▲ seeks harmony
▲ makes judgmental comparisons	▲ appreciates differences
▲ takes everything personally	▲ witnesses with detachment
▲ reacts, often without thinking	▲ mindful of speech and actions
▲ doubtful, insecure, defensive	▲ confident, secure
▲ holds blame and resentment	▲ allows and forgives
▲ stresses reasons why not	▲ sees great possibility
▲ contracted, closed	▲ expanded, open
▲ scarcity perspective	▲ abundance consciousness
▲ needs to control things	▲ accepts things as they are
▲ grievance oriented	▲ solution oriented
▲ missing, wanting something	▲ content and grateful
▲ resists the flow of events	▲ trusts the universal flow
▲ focuses on the past and future	▲ focuses on the present moment
▲ scattered attention	▲ centered awareness
▲ generates suffering	▲ cultivates contentment
▲ motto – "Not good enough"	▲ motto – "It's all good"

Silencing the monkey

There are many ways to silence the automatic mind, some healthier than others. Most people have developed their own ways of controlling or bypassing this chatter. We must overcome its desire to control us and succeed at curbing its influence. We have to keep our monkey on a leash, so to speak. Otherwise, we will never have any peace.

How do you control your Monkey Mind? What methods do you use? You may have that glass of wine everyday after work or take some relaxation-inducing pills or drugs to calm your restless mind. Perhaps you get absorbed in television to quiet your own incessant stream of thoughts.

Or you may have healthier ways of quieting your mental chatter by focusing on your breath or meditating, repeating a favorite saying, prayer or mantra, soaking in a hot bubble bath, becoming absorbed in a hobby, exercising at the gym, going for a walk in nature, writing in a journal, relaxing by a stream or even going fishing. Sometimes I start humming as if I am comforting a baby, because I know that humming takes me right out of my head and into my heart.

A good way to counter the Monkey Mind's negative input is to make up a magic word and use it to shift the negative thought to a positive one. You can use our recommended "Good notice!" to acknowledge yourself for catching the negative thought and then shift to a positive one. Giving yourself a pat on the back for catching the negative thought is much better than punishing yourself with — "Oh, sh_! I did it again."

Years ago it was popular to use a computer metaphor to delete negative comments immediately upon speaking them. When people following this fad said something negative out loud that they did not want to manifest, they would follow it with the statement "Cancel, cancel, clear!" Do whatever works for you.

Whatever techniques you use to bypass or control the automatic mind, the important thing to know is that it is not the voice of truth and it needs to be overcome. The real you, your core essence, must be stronger than this undermining voice. You have to do whatever it takes to bypass the automatic negative thoughts.

Relaxing with breath awareness

A good way to relax your Monkey Mind is to become absolutely still and observe your breathing with your mouth closed. You can begin by following the breath as it enters your nostrils. Close your eyes, and feel your breath flow through your upper chest into your abdomen, expanding your belly. Then slowly exhale, feeling your breath leave your abdomen completely as it exits your upper body through your nostrils. Continue taking similar deep breaths until you feel fully relaxed.

The act of observing your breath can bring you deeper and deeper inside. There are two simple breath techniques I recommend for accessing inner calm. First, exhale more slowly than you inhale. For example, if your natural inhalation is to the count of three, then exhale to the count of four or five. Secondly, you might add holding the in-breath for a few seconds and then holding the out-breath for a few seconds as well. Experiment with what works best for you. Think of your breath as the bridge from your mind to your body and inner being.

As you breathe, observe your thoughts and feelings as if you are an impartial witness. Just allow the thoughts to pass through, without dwelling on them, like clouds gently floating by. A friend once taught me to pretend that my head was a cottage with the windows open. As thoughts buzz into my cottage like flies, I send them right out through an open window and return to observing my breath.

By breathing more deeply and exhaling more slowly, you can increase relaxation and center your attention within. Continue focusing on breath awareness until you reach a point of greater stillness and inner silence. Use your breath to ground yourself in the present moment.

It does take time to learn to quiet the Monkey Mind using breath awareness, and you can succeed at it with practice. You do need to be very patient with yourself and allow your initial experiences to be okay with you however they turn out. The purpose here in this phase of Earth School is to detach from your own superficial ego chatter and access the deeper awareness beyond it, sometimes called your "higher self" or super consciousness.

When you are focused on your inner wisdom, your pure heart naturally practices these principles. As you explore applying each principle in your daily life, see if you can notice the difference between your automatic mind's reaction and your inner knowing.

The journal questions in each chapter may trigger an influx of thoughts and memories. Remember to take a few moments to focus on your breathing to access your inner stillness and clarity. Allow your breath to take you inward before setting intentions for living each principle. Always use your breath to anchor yourself in the present moment.

Three-part exercise to quiet the Monkey Mind

If you are not able to quiet the mind simply by focusing on the breath, a helpful strategy to use is to let your mind ramble for a while. One of the techniques I teach in my retreats is to sit still and allow the stream of thoughts to race through your awareness. Just observe them, label them, and let them go like clouds passing by. Start your meditation time by asking yourself, "What have I got going on in my mind right now?" Then simply scan the thoughts as they pass through without diving into any of them. After a while, you run out of distracting thoughts.

You can also quiet the Monkey Mind by doing the following three-part meditation exercise:

1. *Scan your thoughts: First, scan all of the thoughts passing through. Watch a ticker-tape of them passing by without stopping to engage in any of them. Then visualize yourself at a waterfall or a beautiful place that fills you with joy. Take a deep breath and exhale, letting go of all of the thoughts with an audible sigh.*

Do this three times and then visualize the word TRUST. See the word TRUST written in the sky or behind your closed eyelids. Breathe in the trust that all of the thoughts and concerns you scanned are in the process of being taken care of in this moment. Breathe this trust into every part of your mind and body.

*(2.) **Scan your emotions:** Next, scan all of your feelings. Ask yourself, "What have I been feeling lately?" Do an inventory of all of the emotions that have been passing through you. You may say to yourself that you felt angry when your colleague seemed to be laughing at you or that you felt happy when your neighbor praised your garden. Just scan and label all of the emotions in memory. Take a moment to identify each emotion and let it go like a parade of feelings passing by.*

Continue to scan your emotions until you run out of feelings to label and are complete with the process. Once again, visualize yourself in a location that brings you joy, a powerful place for you. Take in a deep breath, and exhale all of the emotions with a sigh. Do this three times. Then breathe in COMPASSION for yourself and all the other people in your life. Allow your breath to carry this COMPASSION throughout your mind, heart and body.

*(3.) **Scan your physical body:** Finally, scan your body for any places that might feel tight. See if you can consciously bring your awareness to any tight spots and release those areas by breathing into them.*

Pretend that you are an hourglass filled with whatever color of sand you like. What color sand is your hourglass filled with? Start at the top of your head and observe the sand removing all tension from your body as it drains down your glass figure and out of the tips of your fingers and toes.

When your hourglass body is fully drained of colored sand, imagine returning to your joyful location or power spot. Take a deep breath, and exhale with an audible sigh, letting go of any physical tightness, tension or stress. Do this three times.

Then breathe in PEACE, and have PEACE gently flow into all parts of your being. You can inhale peace by visualizing light entering and radiating throughout your entire body — whatever color light you choose — as it flows in, bringing peace to each part from your crown to your toes.

After doing this scan of your mind and breathing in trust, the scan of your emotions and breathing in compassion, and the scan of your body and breathing in peace, your Monkey Mind will be quieter and you will be able to sit in stillness for a while.

It is helpful to frequently scan your mind, emotions and body to keep yourself clear. Often you may pick up feelings and attitudes from other people and situations that can have a negative affect on your energy. I like to use the metaphor of being "a self-cleaning oven." It is good to be in the habit of clearing yourself using mindfulness and the breath. Just as you need to brush your teeth to remove food particles, you need to constantly clear your energy field to let go of whatever negative energies you may be picking up from your surroundings.

In the next chapter, I offer another tool for clearing unwanted feelings and thoughts. It is a four-step process for distinguishing, releasing and transcending whatever might be bothering you. I call this technique for transforming any disturbing thoughts into desired outcomes the "Four D's."

Chapter Three

The Four D's for Transformation

Practice the Four D's:
Distinguish, Detach, Dip and Design

In public school, you focus on learning the three R's, Reading, 'Riting, and 'Rithmetic. Usually you are doing so to meet the approval of your teachers, those who have the power to give you grades and promote you or hold you back.

Now I invite you to practice a series of steps I call the Four D's, not for anyone's approval but for excelling at being the most content you. The Four D's are focal points to help you clear yourself when emotional upsets happen so that you can return to feeling good and being fully present and at ease. They help you transform negative thoughts or experiences into positive outcomes.

When you notice something that you would like to shift, be grateful that it has come to your awareness. Otherwise it might have festered inside of you, creating more problems.

You can begin practicing **The Four D's**:

Distinguish it: Focus on the present moment and whatever is disturbing your serenity right now. Describe it and how it makes you feel. Consciously allow it to be there. Give it your permission. Fully experience it in your mind, heart and body.

Detach from it: Do your best to release any negative emotions you are feeling. See if you can get some distance from the issue. Shrink its importance. Shift to being as neutral as you can about it. Let it go for now.

Dip it in forgiveness, gratitude and humor: The triple dip has you first look at **forgiveness**. See if you can find it in your heart to look at the situation from the other person's point of view and forgive him or her for whatever happened. It is most important to make sure that you forgive yourself for your involvement in the issue. Then move on to **gratitude** and ponder the "silver lining." Find something to be grateful for. Think about the nature of the situation in a more positive way that makes you feel better and lighten up. Ask yourself, "What good can come from this?" Lastly, see if you can dip it in **humor**. Perhaps you can exaggerate what happened to the point of finding it funny and laughable. It really lightens up life when we can make fun of ourselves and laugh at our perceived blunders. (Note: A good way to remember the three dips is to think of the order of the letters in the alphabet — F...G...H... for forgiveness...gratitude...humor.)

Design a new picture: Create the way you want it to be in your mind's eye with vivid sensory detail so you can see, feel, touch, taste and hear it. Design your preferred outcome. Visualize and feel it. Savor it throughout your being.

Delve deeply into each of the Four D's

Distinguish it: Become accustomed to keeping yourself feeling good. Maintain an optimal feeling of well-being as your natural state. When you are centered in your core consciousness and feeling fully grounded, you are open for joy to flow through you. When something causes a shift, and you move away from feeling good, distinguish what you are feeling in that moment and see if you can clear it.

Sometimes things happen that upset you. Someone says or does something you find very offensive, or you are hit with unexpected financial charges that you feel are unwarranted, or you find out very distressing news about a loved one's failing health.

Suddenly, you are pulled off center and tugged by an emotional upset. It's as if you are a fish dangling from a hook.

By "distinguishing it," you allow yourself to focus on whatever you are feeling in the present moment and unhook yourself. You admit that you have that emotion instead of letting it have you or take over your being. You are able to experience the feelings instead of being overwhelmed by them. You acknowledge the situation or issue, recount what happened as truthfully as you can, and describe exactly how it makes you feel now in the present moment. Then you allow yourself to feel those feelings.

Shining the spotlight on whatever is bothering you and telling the truth about your perceptions and feelings is the beginning of clearing it. Once you can allow it to be or accept the way it is, you free yourself from the power it has over you.

While it is necessary to experience your feelings in order to be free of them, you do not want to keep dwelling on them or you will keep yourself stuck. You have to feel the pain that is there to get it out, but you do not want to keep re-living and reinforcing any negative feelings. Fully experience them with the intention of finishing them once and for all.

Remember to distinguish what is present now as opposed to what was in the past. Stay present to feelings that are there for you in the moment as opposed to rerunning familiar tapes of past thoughts implanted in your memory. Take a look to see if there are any old thoughts that you need to uproot and weed out. Whatever you distinguish is transitory. Just the act of witnessing it can cause it to diminish or disappear altogether.

Detach from it: The next step is to stop thinking about the issue and feeling badly about it. See if you can actually drop it from your mind and shift to feeling neutral about whatever happened. There is such a freeing feeling when you just slip into neutral and let go of attachment to having something be a particular way.

For example, if you are serving on a committee and have a strong feeling that something should be done a certain way, that may force you into an adamant position, causing stress and drama. However, you can avoid potential conflict if you decide to communicate your feelings as a "preference" rather than a "position" and consciously coach yourself to remain neutral and open to accepting the committee's ultimate decision. It is difficult to make a persuasive point when you are fixed on a staunch position, but once you let that go, it is easy to successfully communicate ideas from a neutral, non-partial place.

Neutral is a strong stance if you trust that whatever happens will be in the highest good. If it is meant to be, it will come to you. And if it is not meant to be, there will be something else. When you are *neutral,* you are neither for nor against anything. You are simply present without any of the rigid judgments that distort your perception. When you are neutral, you are more aware and receptive to what is happening and more likely to achieve optimal performance.

A fun way to gain some distance from an issue is to imagine putting it in a box and sending it to a faraway location. You can visualize yourself banishing it out of the house or the office. I have imagined putting certain persons on the subway on a one-way trip and watching the doors close as I waved goodbye, smiling.

Find a way that works for you to minimize the distressing situation. You might think of it as simply one grain of sand on the beach of your life. You might consider it one small stitch in the tapestry of your existence. You can imagine that you possess a Magic Minimizer Wand to use anytime you want to shrink a problem. You can wave your Minimizer Wand at challenging times to make troubling incidents become smaller and smaller, less and less important in the scheme of life and ultimately inconsequential. All you have to do is keep waving your wand at that issue until it gets tinier and tinier or until you crack up laughing at yourself waving your imaginary wand.

A helpful way to dismiss the negative emotion is to simply declare, "My peace is more important than this!" and unplug the emotional connection. Another way to move toward taking things less personally is to switch to imagining the other person's point of view. As the saying goes, "you can walk in his or her moccasins" for a while and see if you can experience empathy or sympathy. I have also found it beneficial to repeat the saying "We are all doing the best we can with the resources we have in the moment."

Do whatever you can to get some distance from what is bothering you. If all else fails, go to the movies! Buy some popcorn. Get absorbed in someone else's drama on the big screen. Just know that calling everyone in your phone book to tell your version of the story and get agreement is only going to cause you to spin your tires in the mud and magnify the problem.

If you are still stuck and would like help letting go, there are a number of seminars advertised online that offer techniques for emotional release, and you can always seek professional consultation. Do whatever you can to separate yourself and gain some detachment from the incident or issue.

Dip it … in forgiveness, gratitude and humor (Remember the order of the alphabet — F…G…H… for your triple dip): Get creative now! You have already begun severing the hold this issue has had on you. Now you are holding it in your hands, rather than having it grasping at you, dominating your being. Dig into your imagination and become the director of your own movie. Take a little time to see if there is anything about the situation that requires you to forgive yourself or others. Then, ask yourself if there is anything to be grateful for. Finally, get funny and find some humor in the situation.

The tart strawberry, the undesired situation: Pretend that the situation is a tart strawberry that you are holding in your hand at arm's length away from you. You have a grip on it. It does not control you.

Forgiveness, the chocolate sauce: First, dip the situation in forgiveness, just as you might dip a tart strawberry in chocolate sauce (forgiveness). How can you summon forgiveness for whomever or whatever is disturbing you? How can you empathize with the other person's point of view and be more forgiving?

Gratitude, the whipped cream: Second, dip your chocolate-covered strawberry into a tub of whipped cream (gratitude). What good can come from this? How is it a gift to me? What might I gain from it? What is it here to teach me?

Humor, the chopped nuts: Finally, dip your chocolate-dripping, whipped-cream-covered strawberry in a bowl of crushed nuts (humor). What is the funny part of this? How can I get myself to lighten up and laugh about it?

A fun way to lighten up is to play a game called "It Could Be Worse!" Brainstorm a list of even more devastating circumstances that could have occurred but did not, and this will make what did happen seem much less horrible to you. For example, when I backed into a stone wall beside a friend's driveway and badly dented my brand new car's bumper, I played "It Could Be Worse."

I began thinking that I could have hit another car or a person or someone's pet. I immediately lightened up, realizing that there were no dire consequences, just the expense and inconvenience of getting the bumper fixed. I became grateful that this incident could be resolved by simply writing a check. I imagined how horrible it would have been to have hurt someone and was very much relieved.

Another strategy is to exaggerate your experience to the point of having it become laughable. I was once in a seminar that asked participants to exaggerate painful moments using humor. It was a sad time for me, just after a boyfriend had broken up with me, and I imagined two scenes, exaggerating my despair over his leaving. In one, I was lying prostrate on the floor grabbing his pants leg, screaming "Don't go! I love you. You know I am the one!"

In the second scene, I was in a western movie, wearing a 1900's long dress with a bustle and bonnet. Sobbing hysterically, I threw my body across the railroad tracks, screaming, "Without you, there is no reason to live!" Both scenes had me laughing so hard that they provided a great emotional release and allowed my joy to come through. Do whatever it takes to make you feel better about the situation. And if the issue keeps resurfacing, remember you can shrink it with your Magic Minimizer Wand.

Design it: Now it is up to you to design what you do want. You get to savor your strawberry covered with chocolate sauce, whipped cream and chopped nuts. Take time to luxuriate in the delicious outcome you want to experience. Picture it in your mind with utmost detail. Feel the sensations of having it manifest. Launch the intention to attract it in your life. Instead of just drawing a mental picture, it is important that you work at both visualizing it and feeling what having it will be like. Engage all five of your senses in savoring the experience of having what you want. See it. Feel it. Taste it. Touch it. Hear it.

Let's use the example of having someone end a relationship abruptly. Take time to design the perfect partner and imagine diving into that loving relationship. See your new partner's kind, loving eyes, smiling face and sexy body. Feel the tender touch of your lover's hand and enjoy being immersed in each other at the most romantic candle-lit table in your favorite restaurant. Cherish intimate moments together by the fireplace. Feel the security of being held in loving arms. Go to sleep with this wonderful partner snuggling, warmly wrapped around your body. Summoning that loving, satisfied vibration (after releasing the needy, dissatisfied vibe) will make you feel better and help attract that kind of loving person to you.

Be careful to focus on having your desired outcome rather than on "needing to" have it. Avoid the pitfall of dwelling on the unwanted situation or the feeling of lack. If you are designing the perfect relationship, do not dwell on how lonely it is without a companion. If you are visualizing getting a raise at work, do not focus on how much you need more money.

Remember: You get what you think, and you attract the same

kind of energy you send out. Be a magnet for what you want to manifest by designing it and expressing constant interest in it. Keep that design alive in your experience. Run it repeatedly through your consciousness and your emotions like a movie you are projecting, and watch it appear in your life.

Simply remember to **Distinguish … Detach … Dip … and …Design.** It's a great formula for dealing with the glitches to your serenity. It even makes a good sing-along jingle. Try singing — *"Distinguish/Detach/Dip 'n' Design!"* Have fun playing with the Four D's with the sole intention of making yourself feel better so you can attract the flow of joy.

Remember to practice the Four D's to transform disturbing thoughts

- Identify the situation that has an emotional "charge" on it
- **Distinguish** in detail what you are thinking and feeling about the upset. Experience it fully so you can let it go
- **Detach** from it. Shrink its importance. Gain distance from it
- **Dip** it in F-G-H — **Forgiveness**, **Gratitude**, and **Humor**
- **Design** a new picture with your desired outcome

Don't take your own life personally

As you witness yourself in the process of life, trust what you perceive and ask what you can learn from it. Let go of holding on to old issues, and do not take things personally. Know that at any moment, you can shift to a higher consciousness by simply allowing yourself to think more positive thoughts that make you feel better. Remember to find something to be grateful for or to laugh about. Gratitude and humor can help you dissolve upsets. Most often people are not doing anything to you. They are just doing what they do, and you take it personally.

When I hear someone complain about another's behavior, I often ask for the name of the alleged culprit, and say "David is not doing anything to you. David is just being David." You can fill in the name of your challenging person, and see if you find this statement freeing. The great master Snoopy says that *"Happiness is not taking your own life personally."* It bears repeating that we all are doing the best we can in Earth School with the resources available to us at any given moment. Sometimes we show up better than at other times, but it is all learning.

A chance to reflect on your life with compassion

Now, I invite you to read the explanation for each principle and apply it to your life. Ponder the ways you are already living each code, and think of ways you could practice it more fully in everyday life.

Have a journal handy to record your thoughts. Keep an open mind and a forgiving heart. Be as honest as you can. Tell the whole truth about whatever comes up in your thoughts and feelings. Remember to use the power of the breath to ground you in the present moment.

Be careful not to get into the stern mode of "I should" or "I need to." Explore using the principles more gently, focusing on "choice" rather than "need." Say "I could" or "I would like to." Whatever you do, please refrain from applying these principles to your husband, wife, children, neighbors or colleagues. The codes are optional guides to self-awareness and are not to be inflicted on others as in –"You need to" or "You should."

As you answer the reflection questions, I urge you to accept yourself as being good enough just the way you are in this very moment — even with the things you regard to be your flaws or shortcomings. You are a perfect developing being in the process of living with your human foibles and choreographing shifts toward greater joy. You are aiming to make the best out of life experiences as you learn new lessons and progress through Earth School. You did not come with a manual telling you how to live or raise your children or face the challenges of each day.

Say "Good notice!" and shift

I invite you to use these principles as guides to enrich the success and joy in your life, and refrain from using them to arouse guilt, blame or bad feelings of any kind. I learned from my first Yoga teacher that self-blame is the greatest injury of all. A wise friend taught me to say, "Good notice!" and smile whenever I see something about myself I can shift. "Good notice!" means no judgment, no blame, just gratitude for the new awareness. Let everything go like running water. Whatever you do, trust that everything *is* in divine order.

· Part II ·

*Five Principles for
Social Harmony*

Introducing the Sages'Wisdom

As mentioned at the beginning of Part I, Patanjali recorded our ten life-enhancing principles as practices recommended to prevent human suffering. They appear in the *Yoga Sutras* of Patanjali, Book II., #29-45 of 195 sutras (wise sayings) that had been handed down for centuries by Indian sages. The first five principles address attitudes toward others that are the key to social success. They guide us to develop and maintain a high level of integrity in all of our daily interactions.

A look at the principles for social harmony

In *The Secret Power of Yoga*, Nischala Joy Devi presents Patanjali's five principles for social harmony that "encourage us to live in peace with ourselves and one another:"

1. *"Embracing reverence and love for all (Ahimsa), we experience oneness*
2. *Dedicated to truth and integrity (Satya), our thoughts, words and actions gain the power to manifest*
3. *Abiding in generosity and honesty (Asteya), material and spiritual prosperity is bestowed*
4. *Devoted to living a balanced and moderate life (Brahmacharya), the scope of one's life force becomes boundless*
5. *Acknowledging abundance (Aparigraha), we recognize the blessings in everything and gain insights into the purpose of our worldly existence"*[10]

To make it simple and easy, I have captured the essence of each principle in a few words, stating it as a practice to follow:

1. Practice compassion
2. Be truthful
3. Respect what belongs to others
4. Manage your energy
5. Let go of possessiveness

Let's begin examining how you can benefit from living these principles more fully starting with the practice of compassion.

Chapter One

Practice Compassion

Imagine there is an invisible movie camera suspended in the solar system, recording all of the days of your life on earth. It has been filming each moment you have lived thus far, capturing your every movement and comment as you have been playing out your roles on the stage of life and behind the scenes. What kind of motion pictures would the universal movie camera play back for you? How many scenes would reveal moments you were not quite "an angel" – experiences that you would prefer not to have captured on film?

Yes, the universe's hidden movie camera did film you during all of your most shining moments as well as the times you repeated vicious gossip, made harsh judgments against innocent people and inflicted angry outbursts on unsuspecting victims — at home, in school, at work and in your neighborhood. A quick review of your life to this point might reveal times when you now realize that you could have been kinder and practiced greater compassion for others.

Take some time to silently review such moments. Reflect on which scenes you might choose to delete from your movie if you were given the opportunity to "revise" your life. Appreciate what you learn from reviewing these imaginary movies. Take the lessons with you as you seize this opportunity to start your life's movie over from this moment on.

We are all basically good people. Yet, because we are human, there are times when each of us can be unkind. Whether it's being impatient with a family member, becoming annoyed with a neighbor or getting angry at another driver — there are times when we do not treat those around us with compassion. My theory is that this happens inadvertently when we allow ourselves to be on overload and are not taking care to center and respect ourselves.

Perhaps you tend to overload yourself with more to do than you can compassionately achieve. Maybe you let others demand more of you than you can reasonably accomplish. In what areas of life – with work, family, friends or community projects – do you over-extend yourself beyond what is healthy? How do you forget to respect your limits and violate being compassionate to yourself? Take a look at ways you add stress to your own daily life by demanding too much of yourself and piling on the pressure.

It is vital to start practicing this principle of compassion by being kind and gentle to yourself. Take the time to nurture yourself and refrain from letting the demands of others cause you undue tension and tiredness. Stop allowing external forces to prevent you from practicing self-care and mindfulness throughout each day. If you start to have more respect for your own state of being, you can carry that kindness to others as you make it a priority to lead your life with grace and ease.

The sages' wisdom

In the *Yoga Sutras* of Patanjali, the call to practice compassion is the first and paramount principle to be followed. This means that it is most important to be compassionate at all times even when following the other nine principles. The sages assert that, "embracing reverence and love for all, we experience oneness."[11] They recommend that we express loving kindness to all beings in our everyday speech, thought and behavior.

Sages say that the reward for mastering compassion is that it will make us so gentle and loving that no violence will be able to exist in our presence. The sutra on the benefits of achieving compassion says that "When nonviolence in speech, thought and action is established, one's aggressive nature is relinquished and others abandon hostility in one's presence."[12]

When you have mastered unconditional kindness, anyone intending malice or harm toward you will be stopped by the loving nature you exude. An illustration of this is found in a story about the Peace Pilgrim, who walked more than 25,000 miles from 1953 to 1981 on a personal pilgrimage for peace. She vowed to remain a wanderer until mankind learned the way of peace, walking until given shelter and fasting until given food.

The Peace Pilgrim represents the epitome of a compassionate soul, whose loving heart touched and inspired all who met her. She reported taking a ride in a car with a man who later admitted that he had originally intended to rob and perhaps even assault her. Once in her presence, he was so moved by her love and compassion that he could not harm her. This is the power that the sages claim will develop in you when you become totally compassionate.

Compassion means reverence, trust and benevolence

The first and paramount of our ten guidelines for success is the ancient code of nonviolence or non-harming, which stated positively is "Practice compassion." The meaning of "non-harming" goes much further than simply not committing acts of violence. It denotes a way of being that is unconditionally compassionate and kind.

Practicing compassion stems from an understanding of the connectedness of all living beings. First, we must acknowledge that there is a single source of all we will ever witness in our world. Everything is part of that one creative force or all-being consciousness. Feeling the oneness is inherent in the meaning of the word "compassion." The prefix "com-" means "with," and the root "passion" means "strong feeling." Having compassion means that we experience strong feelings of connectedness with other beings. It is a deep reverence for all living creatures. This attitude of reverence guides us to honor every being with respect and kindness, whether a person, plant, insect or animal.

In addition to expressing affinity with the oneness, the true spirit of compassion involves trusting the process of life. Underlying compassion is the belief that as part of the oneness, we trust in the divine order and timing of the flow of events. We welcome possibilities that are not part of our plan and see everything that happens in life as part of a huge orchestration by the oneness.

Life gives us the experiences we need to learn, grow and develop. Sometimes they feel like painful breakdowns, but they are always breakthroughs to greater growth and well-being. The soul needs challenges to move ahead and evolve, so that's why things shift. It's somewhat like playing a video game in which we master one level, and then we go on to the next.

In the flow of events, we attract what we need to advance ourselves. Life mirrors our quest to know ourselves in all ways and find the balance and mastery we all seek. We draw people into our lives to complement and challenge who we believe we are. The challenges prompt us to know ourselves more fully and achieve a greater level of healing. Those who believe in reincarnation, would add that our life essence is eternal and the lessons of life experiences are ongoing. Whether or not we may believe in reincarnation, we might recognize the possibility that the soul lives on beyond the life of the body.[13] *Becoming compassionate to the core depth of being is the first principle to embrace in our lives.*

Compassion is often defined as "unconditional love." This means loving everyone, however they are in the moment, without requiring them to earn love by meeting certain conditions or standards. Being nice to gain something, to impress someone or to appear to be "holier than thou" is not being authentically compassionate because this kind behavior is conditional and prompted by a hidden agenda.

Compassion is the mindset and heart-space of caring and behaving kindly to everyone, not just those we deem worthy or those who are well-behaved. It means being kind even when others are nasty, rude or drunk. Compassion entails seeing others in their highest good, despite outward appearances. It means being open to understand their point of view, to "walk a mile in their moccasins," and to understand that they are doing the best they can with the resources they have in the moment. Compassion means genuinely caring for other beings with an open heart and a gentle manner.

Exploring compassion and non-violence

Practicing compassion, we treat each being with unconditional love and kindness as an extension of our own selves and never intentionally cause harm or behave violently. Based on the concept that all creatures in the universe are one, whatever we do to another, we do to ourselves. Likewise, what we do to ourselves has a ripple effect on others. In addition, the law of retribution or karma ensures that the kind of energy we put out will surely come back to us, as in the common saying, "What goes around, comes around." The more harsh projections we put on other people, the more negativity we will reap at some point in time when the boomerang we tossed catches up with us.

The crucial part of this code is that it is "unconditional." This means that no matter what we feel might warrant behaving in an unkind way, under all conditions, we must practice compassion. We can make a conscious effort to find common ground with people who seem strange to us. Someone we clash with at work may have children at home who are the same age as ours. We can look for something to appreciate in people we might find offensive.

We can search for a way to summon respect for them. Even our worst enemy might be rooting for the same football team or enamored of our favorite television show. We can intentionally focus on the qualities we all share and appreciate the ways we are all alike rather than judging others based on their differences. Instead of looking through a lens of judgment and blame, we can choose to look through eyes of unconditional compassion.

I once saw a mother yank her little daughter's arm and practically drag her tiny body down the supermarket aisle. "How horrible," I thought, wanting to reach out to rescue the child. At the same time, I could look compassionately at the poor, frustrated mother who had erupted and lost her temper. Both needed help. Although I do not condone her actions, I can see that perhaps if this tired, over-wrought mother could have taken some time from childcare to relax and take better care of herself, she might have had more love and patience available to give to her child.

Gandhi's five elements of compassion

Carrying on his grandfather's teachings, Arun Gandhi writes about the nature of nonviolence in *Legacy of Love*. He focuses on five elements of nonviolence: love, respect, understanding, acceptance, and appreciation.[14]

In a challenging encounter, we can be mindful to look for a reason to *love* or *respect* the other person. We can summon *understanding* and empathy from within our hearts, as I did with the upset mother described earlier. We can learn to *accept* what we do not like about another person and realize that s/he is probably mirroring something we do not accept about ourselves. And we can always search for some way to feel genuine *appreciation* for the other being.

While it may be difficult to appreciate insects that co-exist with us, the interconnectedness of all living creatures calls for us to honor every being. I try not to kill insects if I can help it. I have a jar with a piece of cardboard that I use to remove any spiders from my house. I gently trap the spider in the jar, being careful not to hurt it. Then I cover the jar with the cardboard, walk outside a distance from my house, and let the unharmed spider go free.

However, to be truthful here, I must admit that there have been moments when my compassion has lapsed. Sometimes, when I am stark naked and about to get into the bathtub and see a huge spider lurking in the tub, I may let the water wash him down the drain. But even when I do that, I am conscious that I am washing another life down the drain.

While the goal is to never hurt a "harmless" creature, I think of it in terms of setting healthy boundaries of co-habitation, such as safety first — "I will honor your space as long as you honor mine." We must have compassion for ourselves first, and protect ourselves against the threat of danger from a spider that could be a poisonous black widow or from termites that could chew up the wooden parts of the house. The rule of thumb might be to avoid "senseless killing" and honor all living creatures whenever possible.

The lesson of not killing insects was taught to me by the ants. One day, while I was "trying" to do Yoga postures out on the red rocks, I kept being bothered by ants crawling onto my legs. Well, in one unthinking swoop, I reached down and smashed the ant crawling up my calf and brushed it aside. As I sat up, about to continue doing my poses, I realized I had taken a life.

Seeing the other ants scamper about made me feel deeply saddened that I had mindlessly killed another creature, a beloved member of the ant community. I was so moved by the incident that I went home and wrote a poem called "Requiem for An Ant." Since that day, I have remained conscious to honor the helpless insects even though I do not like them in "my space." Perhaps I was outside doing Yoga in "their space."

In applying the other nine life principles, always keep "practice compassion" as the primary focus. Even when employing the principle of truthfulness or discipline to achieve goals, you must not violate the practice of compassion, which is paramount. Most importantly, remember that practicing compassion starts at home with you and your family.

How do you practice compassion?

First, you must treat yourself with unconditional loving kindness. Then extend that caring out to other people. It is often the promises to yourself that you break most easily while keeping your commitments to others. The bubble bath you were so looking forward to at the end of the day gives way to all the things you need to do for your house, spouse and children. How many times during the day do you berate yourself for something you did or did not do right? Learning to be more accepting and compassionate toward yourself is the first step in developing your innate compassionate nature.

His Holiness the Dalai Lama on contentment and compassion

In the Dalai Lama's new book, His Holiness speaks of our purpose on earth being to achieve contentment and suggests that the way to gain inner tranquility is to develop compassion. The following message from the Dalai Lama is excerpted from his book, *In My Own Words: An Introduction to My Teachings and Philosophy* by His Holiness the Dali Lama (published Sept. 2008):

"I believe that the purpose of life is to be happy. From the moment of birth, every human being wants happiness and does not want suffering. Neither social conditioning nor education nor ideology affects this. From the very core of our being, we simply desire contentment. I don't know whether the universe, with its countless galaxies, stars, and planets, has a deeper meaning or not, but — at the very least — it is clear that we humans who live on this earth face the task of making a happy life for ourselves. Therefore, it is important to discover what will bring about the greatest degree of happiness....

"From my own limited experience, I have found that the greatest degree of inner tranquility comes from the development of love and compassion. The more we care for the happiness of others, the greater our own sense of well-being becomes. Cultivating a close, warmhearted feeling for others automatically puts the mind at ease. This helps remove whatever fears or insecurities we may have and gives us the strength to cope with any obstacles we encounter. It is the ultimate source of success in life."[15]

Thus, His Holiness, the Dalai Lama, teaches us that developing compassion and warmhearted feelings for others is the way to achieve lifelong success and well-being.

Everyday examples

While we consider ourselves generally kind people, there may be times that we forget to be compassionate and reverent to ourselves and other creatures. Everyone gets used to doing things habitually and perhaps almost automatically without thinking. Sometimes we do not see our lapses into unkindness clearly because we are overwrought with tension. See if any of these examples apply to you.

▲ "Kicking yourself" because you said something you think you shouldn't have

▲ Looking in the mirror and judging some part of your appearance harshly

▲ Making a mistake and beating yourself up for it

▲ Spreading negative rumors about colleagues or neighbors

▲ Becoming impatient with slow-moving clerks in stores

▲ Killing harmless insects when there is no need to do so

▲ Getting irritable with family members

▲ Never really listening to a certain person

▲ Carrying resentment for someone's behavior you found objectionable

▲ Judging someone harshly for the things s/he confided in you

▲ Having prejudices against certain kinds of people

"Monkey Mind" protests and reality checks

You may find your mind automatically resisting the notion of practicing unconditional kindness. What is your Monkey Mind saying about practicing compassion? Perhaps it is making objections similar to the following —

Monkey Mind: *I cannot be nice all of the time. No one is nice all of the time. Some people really are irritating, and there are things I just cannot tolerate. Sometimes you've got to put people in their place when they are way out of line.*

Reality check: Being compassionate does not mean being "nice" all of the time. No one is asking you to be syrupy sweet all of the time. Yes, some people really can be irritating! Practicing compassion means honoring others. Sometimes it may mean simply turning politely away and refraining from comment.

Honoring other beings is respecting them. If you are experiencing difficulty, you do not take it out on others by abusing them. Most likely, if you are having a "bad day," you are already being unkind to yourself. When you feel yourself behaving unkindly, you can catch yourself and shift. There is really no excuse for dumping on others.

There will always be people whom you prefer over others because they resemble you. Yet, you can still be kind to the people who are very much unlike you, even to those who "rub you the wrong way." You can refrain from judging them, look for the good in them and treat them with politeness.

I recall wondering about this one lady in a Yoga class who was dressed in a very sexy, low cut black bodysuit with high heeled black boots. She stood out from the others in the Arizona class with her curved fingernails with black polish, almost like fangs, and green streaks in her hair, the emerald color of Saint Patrick's Day. Since most of the students and I wore simple stretch clothes or sweat suits, she just caught my eye and I wondered about her. It turned out that when my car did not start, she volunteered to drive me home. I found her to be a deeply spiritual, beautiful person despite the fact that her appearance had not led me to think we would be kindred spirits and compatible friends.

We have to be careful about judging from appearances. It is human nature to move toward what is comfortable or rewarding and move away from what does not appeal to you. Being compassionate to yourself means you will move away from a relationship, a situation, or a job that does not honor you. *Refrain from harsh judgment. Stay where it feels good, and move away from where it doesn't feel good.*

Monkey Mind: *If someone starts arguing and verbally attacks me, I am not going to just "turn the other cheek." If I am threatened, I'm going to fight back.*

Reality check: You do *not* have to fight back when you are verbally attacked. If someone oversteps your boundaries, you can respond to the situation by communicating your feelings in a respectful way using "I" statements instead of blasting the other person. The key is to stop your automatic reaction to pounce back. If you can interrupt your chain reaction, perhaps you can slow down enough to choose a compassionate response instead of letting your anger run the show.

If you can catch your breath and think of the potential consequences, a brief time-out can help you choose a gentler way to respond to a challenging situation. A good tactic for holding back an emotional eruption is to simply excuse yourself and go to the bathroom. That will allow you to leave the room and have a few moments to compose yourself and think of an appropriate response. Or if the situation allows, let it go for now and choose a future time to gently address it when you have less emotional charge on it. Do whatever it takes to maintain your boundaries appropriately without reacting.

A poem called *Strength*, by Amrit Desai, applies perfectly here —

> Your strength is not in your muscles
> It does not come from
> Fighting negative situations
> Or winning against a negative enemy.
> Your strength is in your calmness,
> In the clarity of your mind.
> Strength comes from
> Putting the negative aside,
> Without reacting.
> Win in calmness,
> In consciousness,
> In balance.
> Win without fighting.[16]

Monkey Mind: *You say not to kill anything. Well, do you expect me to live with ants running all over my kitchen counters or mosquitoes biting my family at night while we sleep? I hate spiders and if I see one, I'm going to reach for the nearest thing to kill it.*

Reality check: The principle of non-violence reminds us to live so that we do not consciously harm any other beings. If your well-being is threatened, you have to make a conscious choice as to whether it is necessary to use violence to protect yourself. Practicing kindness and nonviolence does not mean you cannot stand up for yourself. If you are physically assaulted, you do need to fight back to save yourself. In a life-threatening situation, you have to protect yourself, and that is the only time you must deliberately cause harm. For instance, if your house is infested with harmful rodents, you must take action to get rid of them.

After a workshop I led a few years ago in Barbados, a very sensitive Bejan woman asked my advice about non-harming. She shyly whispered that sometimes rats get into her house, making her fear for the safety of her small children. Following this principle would suggest that this woman use every natural means possible to send varmints away from her premises before engaging in violence against them. Remember to set boundaries for safety and be compassionate to yourself first. In a situation in which health and well-being are threatened, violence may be necessary, but it is a conscious decision to violate the principle of non-harming and respect for life.

Respect others while being true to your own nature

A popular story from the ancient Indian lore called the Vedas tells about a wandering monk who would make a yearly circuit through the villages, sharing teachings of non-violence. One day he came upon a menacing snake that was terrorizing the villagers. The snake took the monk's teachings to heart and radically changed his ways, seldom hissing at anyone.

A year later when the monk once again met the formerly magnificent snake, it was so frail and bruised that the monk could not believe it was the same snake. Asked what had happened, the snake lamented that the children now threw rocks at him and taunted him so much that he was afraid to leave his hiding place. The monk replied that he had taught the snake to practice non-violence, but he had never told the snake not to hiss. You can practice nonviolence while being true to your own self-expression.

No-fault reflection, discussion or journal writing

Take some time to think about how you might practice loving kindness more fully in your own life. Here are some suggestions for exploring ideas, either in thought, discussion or journal writing.

Stream-of-consciousness jottings: Freewriting for discovery and release

If you enjoy writing, you might keep a journal reviewing your practice of compassion. "Freewriting" is simply putting pen to paper and writing whatever comes to you. Record any thoughts without stopping to think about what you are writing or how you are writing it. Forget about grammar or spelling or any audience. No one is to read it other than you.

Jotting down stream-of-consciousness thoughts has at least two benefits: discovery and catharsis. You can see what thoughts and feelings come up and discover things beneath the surface that you were not aware of before writing revealed them. The simple act of recognizing something marks the beginning of creating freedom around it. Writing your thoughts and feelings offers a good way to complete and release them.

Clearing past unkindness

Write a list of the greatest challenges to your serenity in Earth School. Honestly review the instances in which you have been less than respectful to other people or life forms. Review the past with greater compassion for yourself and others. Consciously recall, forgive and let go of any unpleasant past experiences. Use the Four D's and visualize yourself designing a new picture or scene that shifts the energy to a more positive vibration. See if you can discover some common ways you are more like than unlike the people you have found challenging.

Think about, discuss or write responses to some or all of the questions below. This is no-fault reflection in which there is no blame allowed. But if you do notice yourself slipping into blame, please be willing to shift to forgiving yourself and others right away. Whatever happened is already done and gone. Just recognize where a shift is needed. Appreciate that you noticed this need for change. Do your best to let it go. See the shift already taking place in your mind's imagination.

No-fault reflection questions for thought, discussion or journal writing

Ponder your answers, discuss them with someone or jot them down in a journal.

▲ In what area of your life do you successfully practice unconditional loving kindness? Think of what occurs for you as a result.

▲ Recall circumstances in which you have had difficulty practicing compassion and respect? What have you experienced at such times?

▲ What situations "press your buttons"? How do you react when your "buttons are pressed"? How might you respond more mindfully in those specific situations?

▲ What kinds of people do you tend to judge negatively or feel prejudice against? How might you show them more respect?

▲ Describe a circumstance in which you treated yourself unkindly. What could you have done to treat yourself more gently?

▲ Recall an unpleasant occasion during which you treated someone else unkindly. How might you have summoned love, respect, understanding, acceptance or appreciation for that particular person?

▲ Whom do you gossip about? How do the rumors you are spreading affect other people? How might you deflect gossip when someone else initiates it?

▲ What harmless creatures do you kill? Is there any alternative to violence in those instances?

▲ Recollect a situation in which someone was abusive to you.

Explore your feelings about the way that person acted and the way you responded.

▲ Recall an instance in which someone was offensive and you moved away without reacting. What was the effect on the individual?

▲ Reflect upon the one family member who is most challenging for you. How might you practice unconditional loving kindness with this relative?

Practice the Four D's for transforming upsets: Distinguish, Detach, Dip and Design

In the process of answering the reflection questions in this chapter and the following ones, you may come across disturbing experiences that you would like to alter. Whenever this happens, be grateful that the desire to shift has come to your awareness. You can begin practicing **the Four D's (Distinguish, Detach, Dip and Design)** discussed in Part I, Chapter Three, to clear yourself of negative or upsetting feelings that may have come up. Here's an example of how to apply the Four D's to transform a challenging experience —

Current situation: You have just arrived at work, and your boss emerges from his office with his arm around one of your co-workers. He announces that your colleague has agreed to head the new lucrative account that you were hoping to get. You have difficulty congratulating your rival as you feel a surge of jealousy and disappointment.

> **Distinguish it:** As soon as you can, take a private moment to feel the emotions the incident has stirred in you. Recognize that you were caught off guard by the announcement. Realize that you are jealous of both the attention and the opportunity the boss gave your colleague. Take time to recall the moment the upsetting incident happened, what was said and how it made you feel. The simple act of becoming aware of unsettling feelings helps you release the hold they have on

you. Often, just naming the feelings will have them diminish in power or even disappear.

Detach from it: Then, you can do your best to distance yourself from the incident. Do whatever you can to lessen the grip the bad feelings have had upon you. See if you can let go of the jealous thoughts and feelings, drop the resentment and do your best to become neutral about your colleague. Perhaps say to yourself that you will leave the incident at the office when you go home. Imagine putting it in a file or a desk drawer. Decide to be senior to this feeling rather than its victim. You might think, "My peace is more important than this."

Dip it in forgiveness, gratitude and humor: Once you are no longer gripped by the feelings of jealousy, you can be glad that you noticed what made you feel diminished. Think or say "Good notice!" Then practice the triple dip — F...G...H.... First, you can **forgive** yourself for having those feelings. After all, you are only human. Then you can forgive your boss and your colleague, remembering how good they have been to you in the past and reminding yourself that they did not intentionally set out to hurt you. You can become **grateful** that this experience will help you to stay in your power next time another person at the office is praised, promoted or given accounts that you would like. You can think of reasons it is good that this happened. You might find some **humor** in knowing you can either become a green-eyed monster or remain confident in your own abilities. Mull it over in ways that make you feel better and lighten up.

Design what you prefer: Next you can picture yourself genuinely happy for your associate's good fortune in lieu of resenting it. Imagine yourself confidently congratulating him or her. See the two of you shaking hands and smiling, with the boss appearing pleased in the background. Acknowledge yourself for being so gracious and generous. Finally, visualize a new scene at the office in which you are the one being praised for the work you have masterfully accomplished. See yourself standing proudly, wearing your best suit and a beaming smile as the boss acknowledges your outstanding achievement and each of your colleagues comes over to congratulate you.

Compassion means being patient

Whatever emotions come up in your thoughts, discussions or journal writing, please do not be too demanding of yourself. Remember that you are a student in Earth School. Learning to live these principles is an ongoing process. Just having the intention to do so is admirable. Before you go to bed at night, review the events of the day, and ask yourself how well you practiced this principle of compassion. Every morning, vow to practice it more fully. If being mindful of this guideline causes you to be a little kinder to even one person, you are making progress.

Good notices list

Be grateful for what you realized as you pondered these journal reflection questions. Say "Good notice" whenever you see something you would like to shift. Be happy that it has come to your awareness. Make a brief *Good Notices List* of the things you have noticed and are now shifting.

To make sure that you practice loving kindness with yourself, you can start to notice every time you invalidate yourself. Monitor your thoughts and self-talk. If you see any harshness, shift immediately to compassion. At these times, address yourself softly, perhaps calling your self "Honey." Men, who may feel funny calling themselves "Honey," can choose another term of endearment such as "Bud, Dude or Guy."

Potholes to avoid

▲ Lashing out in anger
▲ Verbally dumping frustration
▲ Inflicting your impatience on people

- ▲ Judging and condemning others
- ▲ Initiating and spreading gossip
- ▲ Blaming yourself for mistakes
- ▲ Treating anyone as less than worthy

Tips to follow

- ▲ Slow down your responses (Take that minute)
- ▲ View everyone as a friend
- ▲ Hesitate in the face of a challenge
- ▲ See yourself in the other person's shoes
- ▲ Find something to be grateful for
- ▲ Look for some way s/he is just like you
- ▲ Give the other person the benefit of the doubt

From now on — Let go and relax

It's time to let go of the past and focus on the present moment from now on. Note the names of those people you choose to be more compassionate with from here on, and think of how you plan to treat them with greater respect. Visualize and feel yourself expressing warmth and concern for them as you begin to empathize with their point of view as people who are attending Earth School just like you. See yourself having learned lessons from challenges of the past.

Become still. Close your eyes and take time to center yourself, using conscious breathing to draw your attention inward. Observe your breath as it flows from the tips of your nostrils deep inside into your inner being. With each inhalation, focus on the present moment. With each exhalation, let go of all thoughts and concerns.

Intention-setting and intention-achieved

Ask yourself, "What are my intentions around loving kindness and respect for life from now on?" Take a few moments to remain in stillness and feel the compassion in your heart as you access the silence within. When you are ready, jot down your intentions for practicing compassion from now on. Instead of creating your intentions in the future tense, write them down as if you have already been living them. Instead of stating what you will no longer do in the future, word your intentions in positive terms, stating what you are now doing.

Rather than saying "I will do my best to avoid upsets at work with Martha," affirm "I am enjoying working with Martha these days." To help manifest the intention, visualize yourself feeling good achieving it. See yourself enjoying chats with Martha and appreciating her opinions even when you do not agree. Experience the two of you warmly smiling and respecting each other's ideas. Truly feel that your intention has been achieved — "I am enjoying working with Martha these days."

Whatever your wording may be, remember that you attract what you think and feel. After all, stated intentions are affirmations, and affirmations do not work when they are mere words not backed up by feelings and strong emotion. Intentions that are words without feeling constitute "lip service." Affirm the intended behavior as already accomplished and present now. Think and feel it having been 100% achieved.

If exploring this principle of compassion has made you decide to be a little kinder to others, you are making progress. Keep in mind this quote from Gandhi — *"We must be the change we wish to see."*

Chapter Two

Be Truthful

George Washington is the only person I know of who is reputed to have never told a lie. Witticisms online note that:

> *"George Washington, as a boy, was ignorant of the commonest accomplishments of youth. He could not even lie."* — Mark Twain

> *"George Washington never told a lie, but then he never had to file a Form 1040."*

> *"George Washington never told a lie, but then he was never stopped by a state trooper for speeding."*[17]

At times, our modern society seems to sanction lying. On television survival shows, real life characters lie constantly to manipulate people so they can win the prize. There is a series of TV commercials for an air spray deodorizer that shows the housewife lying to her husband and friends. In one commercial, she sprays the deodorizer and pretends she has spent the day doing a thorough house cleaning, and in another she lights the deodorizer candle and says it is an imported French scented candle. The advertiser must believe that this type of lying would appeal to the mainstream viewing audience.

In everyday life, our colleagues, friends and acquaintances often reach for the quick lie rather than speak their true feelings. Sometimes they cannot say "No" to a request, so they fabricate excuses. Many of us lie about age or aggrandize our roles and accomplishments to create a more favorable impression. Yet, throughout the ages, we have told children about both George Washington and Pinocchio, whose nose grew longer when he told lies, in order to teach them to tell the truth.

Imagine what it would be like if a part of your face changed dramatically whenever you told a lie. Picture your nose growing longer and longer as you give excuses to the state trooper who stopped you for speeding. It might make you stop lying altogether and stick to telling the truth.

How honest are you to yourself and others? On a scale of one to ten, how might you rate your truthfulness? Take a moment to think about it.

The sages' wisdom

According to the sages, the highest virtue is truthfulness in thought, word and deed. Being truthful leads to a life of harmony, integrity and powerful manifestation. The sages tell us that when one "is firmly established in the practice of truth, his words become so potent that whatever he says comes to realization."[18]

They speak of the mind as engaging in five distinct activities: correct perception, incorrect perception, and imagination, as well as sleep and memory.[19] The sages urge us to be aware that what we experience is filtered though our perceptions, which may be valid or inaccurate and possibly even projections and illusions.

What is truth? — What is correct perception?

It is difficult to get a handle on truth because perceptions are so subjective in nature. What we perceive is filtered through our eyes. Our eyes see what we expect to see, what we are familiar with from the past. Our filter of past experiences colors what we perceive as truth.

An anecdote that demonstrates misapprehension is the familiar tale of six blind men feeling different parts of an elephant and likening it to what they associate with that one part, never experiencing the whole. The blind man feeling the elephant's trunk said it was like a tree branch, the one touching the ear likened it to a fan, and the man stroking the elephant's tusk thought he was feeling a pipe. Similarly, often several eye witnesses to an incident do not report it happening the exact same way.

We must remind ourselves that our perceptions may or may not be accurate. Since everything we experience is filtered though our experiential belief system, what we perceive to be true may not be accurate. Incorrect perception may involve twisting or distorting the facts. It could entail judging based on misunderstanding or projecting misconceptions upon other people.

Was the man's friend being rude in not staying to listen to the end of his story, or did he have an urgent reason to leave? Did the woman's employer favor her male colleague, or was she projecting her own jealousy on the situation? Perceiving incorrectly might have any of us unjustly over-react and snowball negative consequences. It could lead to being defensive, deceitful or deceptive.

The wheel of cause and effect

It is important to understand that there is a law of cause and effect in motion and a need to question our own perceptions of what is true. Every action prompts a reaction, and every thought sets a result in motion. We experience life as a wheel of desires creating effects. *Our thoughts create desires ... that prompt actions ... that cause experiences ... that create impressions ... that filter and affect a new cycle of thoughts-desires-experiences-and-impressions.* In every moment of life, we bring our past impressions forth to color each new experience.

Let's look at the filters of a man who wants to be in a relationship. That thought creates a desire to meet someone who fits his pictures. The man's pictures are based on what he thinks are the qualities of a perfect mate. He has been creating these pictures since the early days when he grew up with his parents. All of the women in his life since childhood have left good or bad impressions. Perhaps he wants someone like his mother or someone who is nothing like her.

As he meets new women, he automatically judges them based on these impressions of the past women in his life. He projects his mind's picture onto all of the new ladies he meets, just like a movie is projected onto a screen. Blinded by his own projections, this man may not even recognize the true qualities that the women he meets have to offer.

Questioning perceptions

At times, in Earth School we may misread people's actions and add meaning to their words. We may project motives where there are none and react defensively. It's quite easy to project our thoughts onto others and perceive what we are programmed to see in our mind's eye. Much of what we view is filtered through incorrect seeing or memory of past traumas and fantasy. Based on this filtering, we project onto others, coloring their actions with negative motives. Often we may magnify our perceptions into a full-blown drama.

The sages advise developing vigilant awareness over our thoughts and constant detachment from taking things personally. They recommend practice and detachment as the means to still the automatic thoughts that can take hold of us. The more we become aware of watching what we think, say and do, the more we can develop witness consciousness. We can observe the need to shift, detach from what we are doing and adjust our behavior.[20] We can learn to still the automatic thought patterns if we practice stepping back and examining our assumptions.

To illustrate over-dramatizing, imagine that an elder brother, Peter, learns from his father that his mother has been shopping with and buying gifts for Rick, the younger brother with whom he has a history of rivalry. Peter takes this simple report and views it through the filter of jealousy and competitiveness that he has always had toward his younger sibling. Very quickly it escalates in his mind into thoughts of his mother showing his brother favoritism and of Rick's taking advantage of their mother's good-hearted generosity by manipulating her into buying expensive gifts. Peter dramatizes the event into proof that his mother does love Rick more than she loves him and that Rick is greedy and manipulative.

So what is the truth? The mother was buying something for her younger son and his older brother became envious and projected his own jealousy and fears, coloring both his brother's and mother's actions with selfish motives and agendas.

Of course, when we engage in such drama, usually we are unaware the whole time that we are doing it. The best we can do is to start to question our perceptions. We can learn to give the other person the benefit of the doubt.

The vastness of universal truth

There are many dimensions to truthfulness. This chapter explores the meaning of truth on three levels:

▲ In the vastness of the universe
▲ In our interactions with self and others
▲ Inside our core being

On a universal scale, truth is so vast a concept that it is difficult to capture in words. Truth is the divine oneness that holds everything together. Gandhi said that "Truth is God and God is Truth." Truth is infinite and seems colored only by the human ability to access it at any given time.

Each of us has our own crayons and coloring book to fill in the scenes of our lives as we experience them in Earth School. We perceive things from the subjective point of view that we have built over the years. It is our fortress of constructed beliefs. There are myriad points of view, perceptions and projections through which everyone filters the truth, so it is hard to pin down the absolute truth without anything added.

Our subjective perceptions change as our Earth School lessons come. As we learn, we incorporate the new information and alter our world view. At times, we have strong beliefs about something and we are absolutely certain about them. Then we gain new knowledge and completely shift our beliefs.

Take, for instance, the case of a veteran machine worker who questioned the value of a new policy instituted by management and resisted following it. Then after becoming more familiar with the way it worked, he found it very beneficial. Following his new rewarding experience, he shifted to being a staunch supporter of the same policy he had once been vehemently against.

Such shifts in perception are common as we remain open to new information and integrate it into our mindset. One day's knowing may give way to another day's knowing — apparently a different truth altogether. Thus, as we grow, our perception of truth changes.

Truth in relationships

While the infinite universal truth seems elusive, the easiest truth to grasp is being truthful in our interactions with ourselves and others. This means doing our best to be honest as long as we do not violate the paramount principle of reverence and compassion. It means we do not speak untruths or exaggerations which distort the truth. We do not withhold information that is in the highest good to be known. We do not gossip or allow others to gossip in our presence. Practicing truthfulness means keeping our word to ourselves and others and fulfilling our commitments as honestly as possible.

As we practice truth, we do our best to have our behavior be genuine and honest, devoid of deceit and projections. Being committed to truthfulness also means that we remain open to understanding another's perceptions of what is true, allowing for differences in point of view. Sometimes this may take the form of listening with an open mind to an opposing argument. It means that we take time to listen to and really hear the person we are vehemently disagreeing with at the moment. It entails a commitment to discover common ground when points of view clash. When communicating with others, it is important to both speak and listen to what is true for each other in a respectful way.

However, if speaking a truth will harm another, sages say to remain silent. Practicing compassion, the supreme principle, along with truthfulness requires that we be kind to ourselves and to others and patient with our progress. We do our best to stay clear-headed and remain aware of our feelings, thoughts, speech and actions so that our behavior consistently reflects truth, clarity and kindness.

As we move from lesson to lesson in Earth School, it is vitally important to tell the truth to ourselves and admit any mistakes or conflict on our part. *If there are any past experiences that continue to upset us despite efforts to release them, there are usually two causes. Either there is something we have not told the truth about or something that we have not forgiven ourselves or another for.*

So if an issue continues to plague you, see if there is any detail you might not have told the full truth about or anything you need to forgive yourself or another person for. Telling the full truth and engaging in total forgiveness for everyone involved should clear up any issue. I have found that once I tell the truth about and honestly accept my role in something that did not work out well, the whole thing lightens up and is no longer an issue for me.

Tapping inner truth

In addition to committing to truth in our behavior with others, we have the opportunity to access the truth within. At any moment in time, we can become still, stop our mental chatter, focus on our breath and explore our inner knowing for answers to our questions. By consciously observing the breath coming through the tips of the nostrils, filling the body and then leaving, we can use the breath to still our thoughts and get in touch with our core consciousness. A helpful way to relax and clear the mind using the breath is described in Part I, Chapter 2, page 25. Concentrating on our breath can help us access the truth and inner knowing that can only be found in the silence within.

Through stillness, we can access the inner wisdom that is our individual connection with the universal truth. Everyone is made of this truth. With conscious practice, we can learn to become quiet and check in with our inner wisdom for guidance. When we are in touch with this inner knowing, we are living in harmony and integrity. *Tapping into an inner sense of truth is the way to affirm that what we know to be true is indeed so.*

We can learn to practice looking somewhere inside ourselves (other than in our heads) for the answers to our questions. In my professional practice as a retreat facilitator, often my retreat clients face issues that they are unable to resolve. I always suggest that they become quiet, breathe into their inner stillness and let go of all thoughts. I invite them to pose their dilemma in the form of a yes-or-no question and ask, "Is this a yes or a no for me?"

Almost always, the response to this technique of inner questioning is a clear "yes" or "no." Then the details about how to work out the situation can be discovered by checking into this core knowing. Sometimes the client receives a clear response, but is not ready to act upon it. For example, s/he might need to end a friendship that is draining or even abusive but may not have the resources to take action on that inner knowing. In such instances, it is best to exercise compassion and tell ourselves that we are not yet ready to do what needs to be done. By accepting that we are not yet ready to act, we can seek support and prepare to take action in the future.

"The truth shall set you free!"

On the last evening of one of my retreats, a participant shared her disappointment that the retreat had not helped her decide whether or not to break up with her boyfriend. I invited her outside to sit on a swing with me and share her concerns about her relationship. Then I asked her to answer my questions quickly and truthfully. She agreed and blurted out fast responses as I repeated the same question a number of times — "Why are you with him?"

After hearing several responses indicating that the relationship was unfulfilling for her, I asked her to look within and see if keeping him in her life was a "yes" or a "no." She immediately answered an emphatic "No!" However, as she continued to talk, I could hear that she was not ready to leave him. Her words suggested that she would probably stay with him and wind up punishing herself for doing so afterwards.

I obtained her permission to reflect back to her what I was hearing —

> "So you are in a relationship with someone who comes over for intimacy and leaves when you want him to stay. You try to break up with him. Then when you go out seeking another relationship and do not find one, you run back to him because he is better than nothing. Now you say you probably will go running to him when he calls and you will feel bad about it later."

> "Okay, let's tell the truth about this. You know that this is not a fulfilling relationship, but you are not strong enough to give up the little attention you are receiving. And you don't have to! Is that about right?"

Suddenly, she lightened up and began smiling. In telling the truth, she gave herself permission to have those conflicting feelings. As the adage says, "The truth shall set you free."

I did not advocate staying with him or leaving. I simply suggested that she tell the truth about how it is now and work on building trust in herself. As in this situation, there may be times that our opinions and actions contradict each other. We may be incongruent, saying one thing and doing another. If we are continuing to do something that we think is ultimately not good for us but are not ready to stop it, we must admit that dilemma, to ourselves at least, and get some support to help strengthen ourselves. If my retreat client is going to be with her boyfriend, it would be best to enjoy the time spent with him without berating herself. Recognizing that a shift is needed marks the beginning of having it happen.

Being authentic

Practicing truthfulness is so much more than not lying. It is a commitment to be as genuine and clear as possible. So many times, people can hide behind being confused. It's our job to unravel any confusion we might experience. We may not always know exactly what steps to take or, indeed, have the courage to take them yet, but we can tell the truth about it. Once an issue becomes clear, life has a way of moving toward its resolution. Making something visible is the first step toward healing it.

Above all, we need to tell the truth about our "shadow side." We all have our great qualities and strengths, our "shining" aspects which are bright and wonderful. Then we also have our unwanted tendencies, our so-called "dark" or "shadow" side. This is the part of us that draws in challenging experiences to help us heal and grow. It is our weaknesses, our bad habits, our short fuses, our irritability, our baser tendencies — any and all of the attributes and behaviors that can pull us down.

It accelerates our growth to recognize and admit the issues we are working on as we learn our lessons in Earth School. Yet, we also need to know when we can heal the issues ourselves and when it would be best to seek professional help.

Living truthfulness is a commitment to be true to ourselves as well as to others. It entails a commitment to find the common ground when points of view differ. Being true to ourselves means we inquire into our own needs. We learn to investigate the motivations behind our actions. Why are we doing what we do? Are we agreeing simply to get approval or feel secure? What truly would be best and most rewarding for us? *Being true to ourselves entails both recognizing and fulfilling our personal desires.*

We must learn NOT to say "yes" in order to get someone's approval when we really want to say "no." Some people give in and do things they would rather not do. For example, a friend who wants to go out for Chinese food might give in and go for the usual Mexican food again upon his buddy's insistence. Or a wife might let her husband drag her to another war movie even though she gets tense watching extreme violence and bloodshed.

A person who cannot say "no" might get overwrought with time-consuming tasks that need to be done to please others. We have to discover what our needs are and honor our own preferences. We can learn to express and fulfill them in harmony with others in our surroundings. Being true to ourselves and genuine with others — that is living truthfulness.

Everyday examples

Most of us think of ourselves as "pretty honest" people. However, let's look at some everyday examples of times when we may be unaware of the fact that we are not fully practicing truthfulness. See if any of the following examples apply to you.

▲ Telling lies so that you will not hurt a person's feelings
▲ Saying "yes" when you really want to say "no"
▲ Omitting the part of the truth you would rather not tell
▲ Making excuses for not doing something you committed to do
▲ Getting angry and blaming it on the other person
▲ Having a hidden agenda for doing nice things
▲ Staying in a job or relationship that is not rewarding
▲ Letting someone talk you out of something you know would be good for you
▲ Glossing over your mistakes to make yourself look better
▲ Telling a lie that leads to other lies

"Monkey Mind" protests and reality checks

You may find your mind automatically resisting the notion of practicing truthfulness. What is it saying? Perhaps it is creating objections similar to those that follow. Take a look at each comment in italics and the counter response. See which ones might relate to you —

Monkey Mind: *A little lying is okay. I would much rather lie than hurt a person's feelings.*

Reality check: Lying to be nice — Once you make a commitment not to tell lies, you will find how easy it is to make the truth gentle. For many, lying is a habit. It is just a matter of taking a moment to remember to tell the truth.

For example, if a friend asked my opinion about an outfit before she purchased it, I would tell her what I personally think, being careful to use "I" statements. However, if she asked me if I liked the outfit she was already wearing at a wedding, even if it did not appeal to me, I would find something I genuinely liked about it such as the great color or style. Omitting judgments that might be hurtful in this instance and finding something true for me to say would be honoring both compassion and truthfulness. It is important to be truthful without violating the principle of compassion.

Suppose you love long hair and a friend shows up with a drastically short hair cut, a truthful and compassionate response would be to say, "You know I love long hair, but your short hairdo lets us see more of your face." The truth need not be as stark as all or nothing. You can find a way to tactfully honor the person and still say something that is true if you are committed to truthfulness as well as kindness.

Monkey Mind: *Do you want me to be a party pooper? How can I stop the guys at work from gossiping? It's the way we bond with each other.*

Reality check: Gossiping — Gossip, like lying, is easily stopped when you make a conscious decision to do so. In fact, practicing truthfulness entails being conscious of your speaking and its effect upon others. When you gossip about someone, you prevent them from showing up as they genuinely are. You meet the new salesperson that you have heard is intimate with the boss, and you are not able to think of anything else when you see her. When others meet the people you gossiped about, they cannot help but judge them by what you have said about them.

How do you stop gossip in your life? All it takes is watching for the moment to jump in and say something like — "Let's not pick on Pamela. We all have our moments." Another strategy would be to remind the group about all of Pamela's wonderful traits. Instead of thinking you are a party pooper, your colleagues or friends might think that you would do the same for them if they are the topic of discussion next time.

Monkey Mind: *There are some people I have a hard time saying "no" to, so it's easier for me to agree to whatever it is than to "make waves."*

Reality check: Saying "Yes" when you mean "No" — Sometimes it is easier to agree and say "yes" rather than "make waves." However, that practice builds resentment. I, personally, have found that whenever I agree to do things I really do not want to do, something inside me sabotages them. You are going against your inner knowing when you outwardly agree to something you inwardly disagree with.

There are tactful ways of saying "no." You can learn to say — "I love you and…" then add on what you prefer. You might choose to buy some time by saying — "Let me think about it" or "I am not sure that I want to do that" or "I'll let you know." Sometimes just delaying the "yes" you feel obliged to give will help you be true to yourself.

Another way to avoid being roped into a quick "yes" is to make a counter-offer. Instead of accepting or declining a proposition, you suggest an appealing alternative. For example, if you are asked to help someone move a full household of furniture to a new home, you might say that you are pretty busy, but can give them a few hours one afternoon or let them use your truck. If you are asked to chair a conference, you might give a counter-offer to serve on one of the committees instead. If your teenager wants a new wardrobe, you might offer to buy her one outfit for now. Suggesting a counter-offer is a way of agreeing to a partial yes that meets your needs. It is a way to both honor yourself and accommodate the person making the request.

No-fault reflection questions for thought, discussion or journal writing

Take some time to think about how you might practice truthfulness more fully in your own life. You might choose to do a little free writing, the technique described in the last chapter for non-stop babbling on paper about the topic. Think about, discuss or write journal responses to some or all of the questions below. This is no-fault reflection, in which there is no blame allowed. Be grateful for whatever you notice. Look at how you might shift your consciousness.

▲ In what aspects of your life are you true to yourself?

▲ In what situations do you overlook your needs? How might you change that?

▲ Does your employment situation seem to be your true calling? In what ways might you express your skills and talents more fully?

▲ In what instances do you withhold or alter the truth? What motivates you to be less than honest?

▲ In what circumstances do you not "walk your talk"? How are your actions and speech sometimes inconsistent?

▲ With what people are you not fully truthful? Why is that?

▲ In what instances do you have trouble saying "no"? Why? How might you present a counter offer or partial "yes" in these cases?

▲ Describe a time you vented your opinion inappropriately. How might you have communicated your perceptions more gently?

▲ If you have anything you have been reluctant to communicate, decide whether or not it is best to do so now. One way to decide is to write the person a letter, which you may or may not choose to send afterwards.

▲ Is there someone you refuse to listen to? How might you allow this person to express his or her point of view?

▲ How might you start being more truthful to others and to yourself? Give a few examples.

Now practice the Four D's
to transform any disturbing thoughts

- Identify the situation that has an emotional "charge" on it
- **Distinguish** in detail what you are thinking and feeling about the upset. Experience it fully so you can let it go
- **Detach** from it. Shrink its importance. Gain distance from it
- **Dip** it in F-G-H — **Forgiveness**, **Gratitude**, and **Humor**
- **Design** a new picture with your desired outcome

Good notices list

Be grateful for what you realized as you pondered these reflection questions regarding truthfulness. Say "Good notice" when you see something you would like to shift. Make a *Good Notices List* of the things you have noticed and are now shifting.

Pot holes to avoid

▲ Stop the automatic quick lie

▲ Don't say "yes" if you don't want to

▲ Question the perceptions you are sure are correct

▲ Be careful not to sell out for approval

▲ Avoid tendencies to exaggerate or manipulate the truth

▲ Take care not to block another's self-expression

▲ Refrain from participating in gossip

Tips to follow

▲ Keep your word

▲ Be true to yourself first

▲ Learn to listen even when you don't agree

▲ Give the other the benefit of the doubt

▲ Tell the truth kindly

▲ Tap into your inner guidance

▲ Be authentic

From now on — Let go and relax

It's time once again to let go of the past and focus on the moments from now on. Note any insights you gained from the discussion questions about being more truthful in your life.

Take some time to review what you realized as you pondered these questions and the life experiences they evoked. Notice what came up for you emotionally about being true to yourself and truthful to others. Let it go as best you can.

See if you can learn the lessons that these past experiences brought as gifts of insight and move on. Be honest with yourself and willing to communicate straightforwardly to those who are still in your life.

Take a little time to sit comfortably, close your eyes and relax. Become still and focus on your breathing for a while. Observe the breath entering and leaving your body. Imagine it bringing in new energy and taking away all of the old feelings and experiences. Begin to inhale deeply and exhale slowly. Exhaling more slowly than you inhale is way to increase relaxation. As you use this expanded, slower breathing, allow it to take you deeper within. Let your breath bring you to a quiet place inside where you can access your inner wisdom in silence.

Intention-setting and intention-achieved

Ask what your intentions are around practicing truthfulness as you move forward in your life. Jot down those intentions. Instead of placing your intentions in the future tense, write them down as if you are already living them. Instead of phrasing them as things you are no longer doing, state in positive terms what you are now doing.

To help manifest the intention, visualize yourself feeling good having achieved these intentions. Experience each intention fully accomplished and enjoy how good it feels. Experience how it feels to be true to yourself and fully honor your own experience of life. See yourself being true to your commitments to yourself and others. Visualize and feel yourself living your intentions and compassionately sharing truths with the people involved in your life.

If you are now a little more conscious of being true to yourself and honest with others, you are already succeeding at practicing this principle. Keep in mind these words from Baba Hari Dass — *"You have to be truthful to yourself in your actions, thoughts and speech before you set out in search of Ultimate Reality, Truth or Love."*[21]

Chapter Three

Respect
What Belongs to Others

"You ought never to take anything that don't belong to you —
if you cannot carry it off."
— from *Advice for Good Little Boys,* by Mark Twain

Such is the advice of humorist Mark Twain, who makes light of the human tendency to take things from others, implying, tongue and cheek, that it's okay if you can "carry it off."

Unfortunately, in our society, taking what does not belong to you often seems to be condoned, providing you can get away with it. In current times, we are sanctioning this kind of behavior on a wide number of prominent television reality shows.

Most of us are not thieves and do not blatantly steal from others. However, I suspect that each of us has taken home little things without permission, even if it was just a towel from a hotel. Perhaps we may have stolen the limelight from a colleague, taken the credit for someone else's work or misused time promised to another person.

The notion of "what belongs to us" is debatable when we consider that in the highest vibration, everything is shared in the oneness. We all share everything as part of the universal source energy. How can we separate drops in the ocean and say this is mine and that is yours?

However, to thrive in the third dimension as human beings living on the earth plane with others in community, we need to honor boundaries. Taking a lesson from the birds, we might say that there is a need to respect the ways other people are building their nests as distinct from the ways we are building ours.

Parenting literature is filled with the need for parents to teach their children not to take what belongs to others, as it is the nature of the young child to simply take what s/he wants. Our third principle and newest Earth School lesson focuses on the need to honor what belongs to others, be it possessions, relationships, creative projects or time promised.

The sages' wisdom

This principle stems from the ancient Yoga code of non-stealing, which is also one of the Ten Commandments. To create harmony with others and develop integrity within ourselves, it is important not to steal, or in positive terms, to honor what belongs to others. The sages remind us that each person has the power to manifest whatever s/he may need, so there is no reason to take anything from another without permission. This principle is based on a belief in the universal flow of abundance.

Sages advise us to trust that there is indeed a universal flow of abundance that extends to everyone. They urge us to invest our energy for the highest good of all and believe that the universe will always provide for us. We are to plant seeds and trust that they will come to fruition. Since we each have our own share of good fortune coming, there is no need to be jealous of or steal from others. The ancients assert that great wealth comes to a person who fully honors what belongs to others.[22]

Each of us has our own wellspring to tap into. When we see others prosper, rather than express envy or covet what they have, we can be genuinely happy for their success. At times, we may feel that we are receiving less than our due share of riches. It is important to learn to nip such negative thinking in the bud and shift to a more positive attitude so that we do not attract more lack with scarcity thinking. The secret is to maintain a prosperity consciousness. We need to shift our focus from bewailing what we believe is missing to feeling gratitude for all that we already have in our lives. As we hold positive thoughts about what we are attracting and manifesting, we can be generous to others and glad to see them prosper.

Respecting what belongs to others goes far beyond the physical realm to include the many more subtle ways a person can mis-appropriate energy, such as harming a person's reputation by spreading gossip about him or her. It is beneficial to explore the application of this wisdom in terms of respecting each other's possessions, relationship commitments, creative contributions, roles and time agreements.

Possessions

First, the obvious place to start a discussion of non-stealing is with concrete possessions. While most of us do not rob banks, we do at times take home things that do not belong to us. No matter how small the item may be, if we do not have expressed permission to take it, that constitutes stealing.

We can heighten our consciousness to respect the property of others, be it returning that library book or video, leaving items belonging to a hotel at the hotel, refraining from taking clerical supplies home from work or remembering to give back something we borrowed. I must confess that I still have #2 pencils from the job I left in 1992. Can you recall ever taking home any such items?

We can explore times we may have been jealous or coveted something belonging to another, such as a luxurious car or a lavish home beyond our current means. Instead of seeing only what is missing, we can turn our attention to the many ways we are blessed with abundance and focus on what we *do* have. We can remember to be grateful for the many comforts in our current home environment and for the ease of having the trusty car we already own.

Relationships

A more subtle form of stealing occurs in everyday relationships with others when we do not respect boundaries. We can sometimes squash another's energy or cause a shift in the energy to bring attention to ourselves. This happens, for example, when we might jump in with the punch line of someone else's joke or repeatedly interrupt a speaker.

We can be mindful not to usurp our partner's stories, not to take over center stage at another person's birthday party and not to make advances toward an attractive person who is in a committed relationship. Honoring relationships, we can avoid flirting with our friend's new date or overstepping boundaries to pull the attention to ourselves in any way. At our jobs, we can refrain from taking credit for the work completed by a colleague. If someone mistakenly acknowledges us, we can name the co-worker who deserves the recognition.

Creative contributions

Though the lines may be a bit blurry at times, this guideline of honoring what belongs to others applies to our contributions at work and in the community. There needs to be respect for the authorship of documents we write, the projects we initiate and the events we design.

When I worked in public education, I recall being an assistant supervisor and having my work "appropriated" by a new supervisor who came in to head the department. She put her new heading on all of the original teaching strategy documents I had composed for the department, deleting my byline which had been prominently displayed. She definitely had no awareness of the propriety of respecting my original work.

This is just one of my Earth School lessons, and I am sure some of you can immediately think of several of your own. This kind of pirating is common in organizations, and it speaks to the need for us to honor each other's original creative contributions.

Time promised

Perhaps the most subtle violation of honoring what belongs to others is stealing time. There is the time at work that we use for personal phone calls and emails, the extra-long lunches that include shopping and errands, and the time off when we duck out early to go to the dentist and still get the full day's pay.

If we look, I am sure each of us can find instances in which we took care of personal needs at the expense of a job — be it at the office or home. Many years ago while substitute teaching, I can recall sitting at the front classroom desk folding my Yoga retreat brochures while the students were doing their work instead of walking around the room more frequently to check on them. Looking at it in retrospect, I see that I did not give the job I was being paid for my full attention. Now I would give the job I had taken for the day 100% of my energy — no blame, just a "good notice."

Very often in families, parents or siblings promise to do something with a child and do not honor that time. An example might be the divorced father who drags his daughter along to do his errands instead of giving her quality time during the one weekend they have together. Another illustration is the person who is always late and makes everyone wait for him or her.

These are just a few examples of not honoring others in daily interactions in Earth School. How well have you established your own boundaries? How can you become more respectful of the boundaries of other people?

Everyday examples

While I am sure that most of us do practice respect for what belongs to others, it's beneficial to explore any areas in which we might shift to having greater respect. Let's look at some common examples of times when we may be unaware that we are not respecting what belongs to others. See if any of these examples apply to you.

▲ Bringing things home from the job without permission
▲ Taking credit for something you did not do
▲ Cutting off or interrupting the person speaking
▲ Flirting with someone else's committed partner
▲ Copying someone's work and saying it's your own idea

▲ Stealing the spotlight from the host of an event

▲ Using time on the job for personal purposes

▲ Not spending time promised with a loved one

▲ Borrowing something and not returning it

▲ Taking more than your share of anything

▲ Sampling store candy or snacks you did not pay for

"Monkey Mind" protests and reality checks

What is your Monkey Mind saying about respecting what belongs to others? See which of the following remarks relate to you —

Monkey Mind: *Give me a break. The office won't miss the paper clips, and the hotel surely will not notice that one towel is gone. Don't make a federal case out of such a little thing.*

Reality check: Taking little things home — There is no need to make a "federal case" out of taking supplies from the office. The intention here is simply to heighten future awareness that "helping yourself to stuff" constitutes stealing. It's fine to take things home with the boss' permission, and it takes only a moment to ask. Your employer will probably appreciate that you asked. If it does not feel right to ask, then you know it is not appropriate.

As for me, I did confess to still having in my possession packages of pencils that I took home from a school position in 1992. When a workshop participant suggested I return them, I replied that rather than book a flight to NYC to return them, I preferred to learn from the experience and refrain from doing it again. Imagine what havoc it would create if each of us went to our desks and closets and attempted to return the things we had taken home without permission throughout our lives!

However, do return any items you come across that you can easily give to the rightful owner. For example, when I moved recently, I discovered a book and a CD that belonged to two of my Yoga teacher colleagues, and I made a point of returning them with a nice note. Let's just be more conscious to respect the property of others in the future.

Monkey Mind: *At work, the person given the assignment is always the one thanked. There is no need to make a big deal about giving credit to those who did the work.*

Reality check: Giving credit where it is due — Yes, a project manager is usually the one who receives credit for a job well-done by staff. Nevertheless, it takes only moments to acknowledge those who did most of the work. Especially in a case in which you are being unjustly praised, you might easily correct the situation by saying that someone else deserves the appreciation as well. A pat on the back or a kind word of acknowledgment to the boss would be ways to show appropriate gratitude. Rather than diminishing yourself in the employer's eyes, transferring the credit to the rightful owner might make the boss value you even more.

Monkey Mind: *Everybody makes calls and checks emails from work and sometimes leaves early. It is expected and goes with the job.*

Reality check: Using office time for personal business — Just because everyone does it, that does not mean it is proper policy. There is probably a margin of personal time allowed in every job situation, depending upon the employer and supervisor. It might be appropriate and perhaps expected for you to check your own email at work and make a few phone calls. You know what is okay with your boss and what would not be appreciated.

The intention here is to raise consciousness about being appropriate with time designated for the job. When you take time from work for your own stuff, you are doing just that — "taking the boss' paid time." It's best to check in with your employer for permission when using a block of paid time for something personal. Asking permission would probably raise your estimation in your boss's eyes and enable you to relax more with the personal use of work time.

No-fault reflection questions for thought, discussion or journal writing

Take some time to reflect upon how you might honor what belongs to others more fully. Think about or jot down responses to your choice of the reflection questions below.

▲ Was there any time you were given undeserved credit for something that others accomplished? How might you have acknowledged the person(s) responsible for the achievement?

▲ How have you misused or mismanaged what belongs to others? What might you do to correct this?

▲ Make a list of anything you borrowed that needs to be returned. Jot down any intentions to return such articles as appropriate.

▲ Take a few moments to think about any items that you took home from a job, hotel or any other source without permission. Note any instances in which you would refrain from taking such things in the future.

▲ Reflect on times you may have used paid job time for personal uses. How much of this was with your boss' permission? What behavior, if any, might you change?

▲ Can you recall any time you may have taken someone's creative ideas without acknowledging him or her? What could you have done to be more appropriate?

▲ Is there anyone whose good fortune you have been jealous of? Picture that person and visualize being truly happy for him or her and content with your own life.

▲ Think about any times you felt overshadowed by another person and strove to be the center of attention. What might you have done differently to honor that person?

▲ For situations involving jealousy or coveting, think about what makes you have such feelings. Ask yourself what you need to alter to release those emotions.

▲ In what relationships, if any, do you tend to dominate, interrupt or inhibit another's self expression? How can you shift to invite the other person's contribution?

▲ Whom have you promised to spend time with and then used the time for other purposes? Explore your reasons for doing this and possibilities for change.

Now practice the Four D's to transform any disturbing thoughts

- Identify the situation that has an emotional "charge" on it
- **Distinguish** in detail what you are thinking and feeling about the upset. Experience it fully so you can let it go
- **Detach** from it. Shrink its importance. Gain distance from it
- **Dip** it in F-G-H — **Forgiveness**, **Gratitude**, and **Humor**
- **Design** a new picture with your desired outcome

Good notices list

Be grateful for what you realized as you pondered the reflection questions about not stealing. Remember that this is no-fault reflection, in which there is no blame or harsh judgment allowed. Simply say "Good notice!" whenever you see something you would like to shift about respecting what belongs to others. Make a brief *Good Notices List* (either in your mind or on paper) of the things you have noticed and are now shifting.

Pot holes to avoid

▲ Taking excessive job time for personal uses
▲ Carelessly taking home company property
▲ Coveting your friend's possessions or relationships
▲ Not honoring people's boundaries
▲ Accepting credit you do not deserve
▲ Interrupting when anyone is speaking
▲ Dominating by stealing the limelight

Tips to follow

▲ Give credit where it is due
▲ Get permission to take anything home

- ▲ Avoid using paid job time for personal needs
- ▲ Respect whoever is speaking or leading
- ▲ Honor others by giving them the time promised
- ▲ Respect the relationships and creations of others
- ▲ Acknowledge the source of original ideas

From now on — Let go and relax

It's time to look at how to incorporate the new awarenesses in your daily life from now on. Review the messages that these past experiences brought as you contemplated non-stealing and respect for what belongs to others. Feel grateful for the understanding you have gained. Use these insights to be more respectful of the possessions, relationships and accomplishments of the people in your life.

Sit comfortably and close your eyes. Take a deep breath and exhale, releasing any emotions with an audible sigh! Do this as many times as you inhale and still feel the need to let go of pent up feelings by exhaling with a big, hefty sigh of release. Sighing out loud in a long exhalation is another technique for releasing anxiety and deepening relaxation.

Intention-setting and intention-achieved

Ask yourself what your intention is concerning establishing and respecting boundaries. Take a few moments to become still and set specific intentions for honoring what belongs to others. State each intention clearly in positive terms using the present tense as if you are already experiencing it. Then both think and feel it happening. Enjoy the feeling of having already successfully achieved it. Then move on and do the same process with the next intention until you are complete.

Imagine experiencing those specific intentions with particular people in your life. Visualize their faces and see yourself showing more respect in terms of their possessions, accomplishments, relationships and time commitments from now on. See yourself being aware of people's boundaries and respecting them. Experience feeling happy for the success of your friends and colleagues. Focus on feeling the fullness of life and appreciate the abundance in your life and in the lives of those around you.

If you are now a little more conscious of being respectful of people's boundaries and honoring what belongs to them, you are already living the wisdom of this principle. Keep in mind this quotation from Sri Swami Satchidananda — *"If we are completely free from stealing and greed, contented with what we have, and if we keep serene minds, all wealth comes to us."*23

Chapter Four

Manage Your Energy

Wouldn't it be great if we could bottle "life force energy" and take a few slurps when needed? We could be like "Popeye the Sailorman," chugging down that can of spinach and becoming more robust just in time to face the next challenge. At least, Popeye knows when he needs to refuel with that can of spinach. Do you?

Prana or life-force

While we live in a physical body composed of organs, blood vessels and cells, we are also composed of an energy or life-force that is called "Prana" in Sanskrit. According to BKS Iyengar, this life-force or Prana —

> "permeates each individual as well as the universe at all levels. It acts as physical energy; as mental energy, where the mind gathers information; and as intellectual energy with a discriminative faculty, where information is examined and filtered. The same prana acts as sexual energy, spiritual energy and cosmic energy. All that vibrates in the universe is prana: heat, light, gravity, magnetism, vigor, power, vitality, electricity, all beings and non-beings. It is the prime mover of all activity. It is the wealth of life. This self-energizing force is the principle of life and of consciousness. It is the creation of all beings in the universe. All beings are born through it and live by it…. Prana is the fundamental energy and the source of all knowledge."[24]

How can we maintain a steady stream of this life force energy? Through conscious breath control, we can increase the amount of prana or life force that we breathe in. By increased monitoring of how we use our energy, we can learn to choose activities that replenish energy and steer away from those that drain it.

This fourth principle teaches us to control and channel our life force energy by practicing moderation and balance. Our energy is our most precious commodity. It is important to conserve our life force energy and direct it to the most beneficial uses. We can learn to respect ourselves enough to keep in mind that our vital energy needs to be regenerated. We can become alert to the ways we squander and renew our own life-force and choose to replenish it. As we become accustomed to checking on our energy level, we can alert ourselves to adjust our energy intake and expenditure when it is about to be depleted.

The sages' wisdom

This principle of energy management stems from the ancient principle called "Brahmacharya." This Sanskrit term denotes the first of four stages of traditional Indian life, whereby students remained celibate to the age of twenty-five as they focused on studying scriptures and learning skills. It was believed that sexual continence would increase the life force channeled to higher goals.

In modern times, this principle stands for the ideal energy balance achieved through moderation. It has come to mean proper conduct, conscious sexuality, moderation of sensual desires, energy conservation and channeling energy to higher purposes.

Sexual energy is a very powerful expression of the life force, and the sages teach that abstinence can help us channel that force of energy toward greater accomplishment. While almost all of the yogis married and had families, they also chose periods of abstinence to conserve and direct their sexual energy into achieving higher goals.

The sages assert that such abstinence or control in no way diminishes the enjoyment of pleasure when we do engage in sexual activity. This does not mean that we have to avoid sex. Instead, it urges us to be conscious about engaging in sex and not allow excesses to dissipate our vital energy. When we are able to be moderate and conserve more life-force, the sages say that great knowledge, vigor, valor and energy flow to us.[25]

We learn from Tantric practices that sexual union can be a conscious channeling of energy between those engaged in the exchange. Sexual intercourse can be entered into with the sacred intention for two beings to be united in their highest consciousness. We can view the sexual union as a sacred interaction and practice "conscious" sexuality rather than indiscriminate sex.

Monitoring and managing our energy

I invite you to look at how you use your sensual and sexual energy and become more conscious of how you expend your life force. Following this principle entails exploring ways you could better manage your energy. For example, could you practice greater moderation with the intake of food, alcohol, coffee or chocolate? How talkative, how active or how lazy are you at times? How much television do you watch? How many hours do you fritter away at the computer? What do you generally do with most of your free time?

Which activities and what people tend to boost and replenish your life-force? Maybe you are energized by doing physical exercise or by being with your most loving friends. In contrast to these uplifting experiences and persons, which actions and people usually drain your energy? Perhaps you are depleted by over-eating or having to endure complaining colleagues.

Everyday examples

Now begin to look into the specific circumstances of your life. Where do you have a need for moderation and balance? Skim the following examples. See if any of them relate to you.

▲ Being too tired to listen to your family or friends talk
▲ Being too zoned out at day's end to take care of yourself

- ▲ Overeating to reduce stress
- ▲ Consuming excessive alcohol to numb yourself
- ▲ Spending hours absorbed in the computer or television
- ▲ Promising yourself to do what's good for you and not following through
- ▲ Over-committing your time to others
- ▲ Starting a lot of projects and not finishing them
- ▲ Not being able to slow down when you need to
- ▲ Having sexual experiences that are less than sacred
- ▲ Not heeding the signs when your body is not doing well
- ▲ Getting caught in emotional dramas that are draining

"Monkey Mind" protests and reality checks
What is your Monkey Mind's immediate response to these ideas about managing your energy and sexuality? Perhaps it is creating objections similar to the ones below. Take a look at each comment in italics and the counter response. See which ones might apply to you —

Monkey Mind: *You cannot expect me to sublimate my sexuality and deny my bodily needs.*

Reality check: Denying bodily needs — No one is suggesting that you sublimate your sexuality, but that you simply express it consciously with great respect for the interchange of energy. The idea is to heighten your regard for sexual expression and hold the act as a sacred union. The sages are suggesting that excessive, unconscious sexuality diminishes energy. At times when you are focused on pursuing higher goals, continence might provide greater energy toward achievement of success.

For example, if you are training for a sports event or about to lead a large seminar, you may find it beneficial to abstain from sexual activity in order to channel all of your energy toward a successful performance. Or if it is best for your energy, have conscious sex with your loved one the night before. You get to monitor your own energy and make your own decisions. The intent is simply to increase awareness and appropriateness. You always have dominion over your sexual expression, providing it is with permission of the other party involved. You might shift to viewing deferred sexual gratification as a way of heightening the importance and power of the sacred act rather than sublimating it.

Monkey Mind: *How do you expect me to conserve energy at work when the job demands are exhausting?*

Reality check: Conserving energy at a demanding job — There are many ways to conserve your energy when your job demands are exhausting. First, practice time management strategies. Learn to prioritize tasks by what needs to be done soonest. Learn to sort tasks into those you must do yourself and those you can delegate responsibly. If you delegate, you must follow up and make sure that the people you delegated tasks to are capable and responsible.

Learn to take stock at the end of the day and prioritize for the next day. If you know that you will always have more work than you can complete in one day, learn to whittle your giant workload down into chunks that can be accomplished today and those that can wait for tomorrow or be given to someone else to do. Take a look and see if there are any time-consuming jobs you are insisting on doing yourself when someone else could be asked or paid to do them.

In addition to practicing time management, it is good to take "transition breaks." When you move from one task to another, you can take a few moments to acknowledge what you have accomplished and relax for a moment before you move on. Before rushing to call clients after checking email, you can take a few minutes to acknowledge yourself. Congratulate yourself for having been able to respond to all of the important emails. Enjoy a few seconds to feel complete with that aspect of your work, and relax your pace instead of moving on hurriedly to the next chore at hand.

Pacing yourself in this way can help you conserve and replenish energy. That pause between emails and calls can also be an opportunity to drop into the stillness inside. That way when you do make your calls, the energy will come from the peace within rather then from a harried person with a long list. I call these moments "drop-ins" and encourage you to take them frequently during your day.

Lastly, rather than rushing to complete the last thing on your list when the clock says it's time to quit, make a note to do it first thing tomorrow. Give yourself a break and a pat on the back. You cannot change your workload, but you can change your attitude toward it and give your well-being some importance. The paramount principle of compassion and reverence for all living beings starts with having respect for your own life force.

Monkey Mind: *There just isn't enough time in the day to get everything done and still have time to do the things I know are good for me.*

Reality check: Not enough time to do things that are good for me — While time does seem to speed by, there is always time to do things that are good for you. There may not always be as much time as you would like for the long version, but you can always manage to touch base with the things that nurture you.

If you don't have time to go on a long hike, take a leisurely walk around the block and enjoy being in the fresh air. If you cannot manage an hour working out at the gym, take twenty minutes to exercise at home. If you cannot get to a Yoga class, take a few moments to do a couple of stretches that you know how to do on your own.

If you don't have a lot of time to curl up with a good book, read to relax for a short while at bedtime. Even if you come home late from work, you can take a little time to connect and be close with your mate and your children. It does not take a lot of time to check in with them and exchange loving support. And if you feel the time spent doing these things was not enough, enjoy the taste of them and plan to give more time to them the next day or on the weekend.

No-fault reflection questions for thought, discussion or journal writing

Take some time to think about how you might practice moderation more fully to balance your energy. You might choose to do a little free writing about this topic — the technique described earlier for non-stop babbling on paper. Think about or jot down responses to some or all of the questions below. This is no-fault reflection, in which there is to be no blame or even mild self-recrimination of any sort. Be grateful for whatever you notice. Look at how you might shift your thinking and your current practices to maximize your energy.

▲ What goals would you pursue if you had more energy?

▲ What areas of your life get neglected when your energy is low?

▲ What is the biggest energy drain in your life, and how might you overcome that?

▲ How do you sometimes overindulge in sex or sensual cravings?

▲ Reflect upon any time you may have used your sexual energy unconsciously.

▲ How might you be excessive with food or alcohol?

▲ How do you sometimes squander your energy in unrewarding ways?

▲ What do you do to conserve and replenish your energy?

▲ In what ways do you use your energy in loving service to others?

▲ Think about areas of excess in your life you would like to reduce. Create a plan with a time frame and a reward for compassionately weaning yourself of one excess.

▲ Draw a circle and create pie slices to show how you use your energy. For example, create a pie wedge for the percentage of time you spend on work, exercise, chores, entertainment, family, relationships, etc. Examining your energy pie, what does it show you about how you use your energy?

Now practice the Four D's to transform any disturbing thoughts

- Identify the situation that has an emotional "charge" on it
- **Distinguish** in detail what you are thinking and feeling about the upset. Experience it fully so you can let it go
- **Detach** from it. Shrink its importance. Gain distance from it
- **Dip** it in F-G-H — **Forgiveness**, **Gratitude**, and **Humor**
- **Design** a new picture with your desired outcome

Good notices list

Once again it is time to let go of all past thoughts and focus on the present moment. What realizations have you gained from the reflection questions about managing your energy? Take the next few moments to review what you noticed as you responded to the reflection questions.

Be grateful for what you realized about your use of energy as you pondered these questions. Remember to say "Good notice!" whenever you see something you would like to shift. Create a mental or written *Good Notices List* of the things you are presently shifting to maximize your energy.

Potholes to avoid

▲ Don't pursue all of your sensual cravings

▲ Stop eating before you are full

▲ End work before you are exhausted

▲ Refrain from taking on more than you can do

▲ Avoid re-running negative experiences

▲ Resist getting sucked into the television

▲ Beware of wasting your energy

Tips to follow

▲ Pace yourself to conserve energy

▲ Take frequent pauses to nurture yourself

- Conserve energy for conscious sacred sexuality
- Choose relationships that are not clinging or draining
- Eat and drink to less than full capacity
- Take vacations to prevent burnout
- Learn to ask for support when you need it

From now on — Let go and relax

Once again it's time to let go of thoughts of the past and shift your awareness to integrating what you are learning about managing energy from now on. Allow whatever came up for you in your thoughts and feelings to be fine for now and relax into the present moment. Be here now and let it all go.

Sit comfortably in a quiet place. Close your eyes and focus on your natural breathing. The next time you inhale, hold the breath in for a few seconds. Then exhale very slowly and hold the breath out for a few moments. Repeat this breathing exercise and holding pattern several times. Holding the in-breath and the out-breath for a few seconds will help you quiet the mind and access your inner being.

Continue breathing naturally. Observe the breath as an energizing organ as it brings in new life force with each inhalation and carries away old feelings with each exhalation. Allow your breath to grow deeper and draw you into a place of silence within. In the stillness, be thankful for what you have understood. Experience yourself as an energy body and get in touch with your expanding consciousness. See yourself showing greater respect for your own vitality as you monitor it and replenish it, making changes for the better.

Intention-setting and intention-achieved

As you focus inward, ask what your intentions are around practicing moderation and conserving energy. Think about or note those intentions. Visualize and feel yourself living each and every intention and consciously managing to keep your energy replenished in your life from now on. Feel that you have achieved and are savoring each intention. Feel yourself having the energy to do everything you have to do with lots of time and energy to do the things you love to do. Enjoy being fully and totally energized and alive.

If you are now a little more conscious of curtailing excesses and creating greater balance in your life through moderation, you are making progress living this principle. Keep in mind these words from TKV Desikachar about managing your energy field — *"At its best, moderation produces the highest individual vitality. Nothing is wanted by us if we seek to develop moderation in all things. Too much of anything results in problems. Too little may be inadequate."*[26]

Chapter Five

Let Go of Possessiveness

By now, I am sure you have heard the story about the monkey who got his hand caught in the jar because he would not let go of the banana. All he had to do was simply let go of the banana, and he could have freed his hand and arm from the jar. Instead, he clung to his object of desire at the expense of his freedom. The point of this story is to look at the "bananas" we cling to at the cost of our freedom.

What are your "bananas"? Are you attached to making something happen that is just not flowing? Are you insisting on certain outcomes instead of allowing things to unfold however they do? Are you collecting too much clutter with closets full of hoarded stuff that you are not using? Are you grasping at any relationships that could use more space? Are you clinging to any friends or perhaps being somewhat controlling with your mate? If the answer to any of these questions is "yes," this fifth principle of non-attachment and non-hoarding can benefit you.

The sages' wisdom

The sages recommend letting go of attachment to people or things. They advise keeping only what we need in the present moment and trusting the universe to provide more when it is needed. Clinging to people or hoarding possessions does not bring happiness. There is a vicious cycle set in motion when attachments cause desire or longing. This creates suffering. Either we yearn for material things and exclusive relationships, or we cling to the ones we have for fear of losing them.

In both instances, the desire to possess things or control people places attention on what is missing and keeps our energy focused on the deficiency. The more attention we give to what we are wanting, the more energy we are sending to the universe to keep it lacking. When we dwell on what's missing, we often succumb to negative emotions of fear, greed and lack instead of shifting our consciousness to being satisfied now and welcoming greater abundance.

Practicing non-hoarding and non-attachment does not mean that we cannot have nice things. It's a matter of not clinging to or hoarding them. We can trust in the flow of material and spiritual abundance and allow material possessions to come and go with an open hand.

The sages claim that when we are totally free of greed and possessiveness, each of us will gain insight into our past and greater understanding of our personality.[27] Without being pulled by desire for more possessions, each of us can focus within to discover the deeper meaning of life.

Trusting in the flow of abundance

It is important to believe that there is a flow of abundance and trust life to bring a share of it our way. This is the fundamental belief underlying the principle of non-hoarding. There is no reason to hoard. Whatever it is that we are hoarding, sages recommend that we only take as much as we can use now and trust that when we need more, it will be available to us. Just when funds might seem to be getting low, there is often another opportunity coming our way if we are open to seeing it.

Personally, I plant seeds and then trust that I will be taken care of. I recall returning home after a summer camping on Mt. Shasta many years ago, not knowing where the money for the rent was going to come from. While I slept in my van's bed at a rest stop, an elderly driver hit the back of my bumper, badly denting it. I awoke with a jolt, but was very gentle and kind to the elderly gentleman, who was extremely upset. We exchanged phone numbers, and I told him I would research the cost of repair and call him.

The next day I told him both the prices for repair and replacement of the bumper. He said that since I had been so kind, he would pay the larger sum to replace the bumper providing I would send him a letter releasing him from any damages, which we both promptly did. I found I could easily live with a dented bumper and was very happy to have the rent money magically appear. Of course, I asked God to please have the money flow in more gently in the future.

In recent times, it sometimes happens that the retreat I have scheduled may not fill but a request comes in for a custom group activity that is even more rewarding. It is truly a matter of faith in the abundance we are attracting. It often comes in ways other than those we have planned. The sages recommend trusting in the abundance of the universe no matter what it looks like at any given moment, especially in times of scarcity.

How much stuff do you hoard?

This principle of non-greed and non-hoarding sheds light on the need to look at what is really important in our lives. It guides us to look at the ways we expend our energy and resources in amassing material goods instead of focusing that energy on our life's purpose. Wordsworth pointed this out in his famous line of poetry, *"Getting and spending, we lay waste our powers. Little we see in nature that is ours."*

Following this principle, you might explore how much "stuff" you hoard. Do you have closets full of seldom-used clothes or shoes? Do you work hard for a paycheck and then spend it on amassing more possessions? Is your life about getting more, bigger, better material things like designer outfits, extravagant houses and fancy cars?

What material things do you think will bring you happiness? What is your attitude toward the possessions you already have, the roles you play and the people you interact with? Do you really trust that your efforts will be rewarded and your basic needs will be provided for in the natural flow of abundance? Is it truly necessary to stockpile provisions for that proverbial rainy day?

The late comedian George Carlin has a very famous comedy routine making fun of how we gather stuff, then need to buy more furniture to hold our stuff, then bigger houses to hold all of the furniture full of stuff, and it goes on and on until we have to write wills to let others know what to do with our stuff when we die!

In what ways are you possessive with people?

Turning from material objects to people, let's take a look at our relationships to see where we might be possessive or clinging. We might examine ways each of us is sometimes possessive of our relationships, not wanting to share them with others. Perhaps we have a growing teenage daughter we would like to keep all boys away from, a favorite secretary at the office that we would like to work only for us, or a relationship partner whose whereabouts we would like to monitor all of the time. Recently, I heard a TV soap opera husband tell his wife, "I let you become a nurse, didn't I?" Now there's a perfect example of being controlling in a relationship.

It takes a tremendous amount of energy to be possessive and attached, and it sometimes prevents people from seeing the real nature of the person or thing they blindly cling to. There are far too many people who remain in abusive relationships with partners they feel attached to, and they don't allow themselves to see how detrimental these relationships are. The movies, media and local gossip mills depict a wide range of unhealthy behaviors in which people are enablers, stalkers or abusers, who are verbally and physically violent to alleged loved ones.

It is quite human to want to hold onto what is precious to you. However, it is important to practice loving and appreciating others without being clinging or controlling. The more we want to hoard and cling, the less satisfied and content we are in the present moment.

Everyday examples

This is a good opportunity to examine the objects and people you cling to and explore ways to let go and streamline. Take a few moments to review the follow examples of hoarding. See which ones, if any, apply to you.

▲ Storing more provisions than you can consume
▲ Charging material possessions you cannot afford
▲ Living in a bigger house than you actually need
▲ Purchasing surplus clothing, bedding and household items
▲ Hoarding stuff because it's on sale
▲ Buying high-priced name brands for show
▲ Owning more vehicles than you need
▲ Refinancing your house for money to buy more things
▲ Keeping a garage or storage unit full of stuff you are not using
▲ Being jealous and clinging toward people in your life
▲ Staying in unfulfilling or abusive relationships

"Monkey Mind" protests and reality checks

What is your Monkey Mind saying about possessiveness and hoarding in your life? Explore your own thoughts and the Monkey Mind's comments below to see what insights they may hold for you —

Monkey Mind: *I work very hard to build a good life for my family. Don't tell me not to want a great house, a nice car and the best that money can buy!*

Reality check: Having a great house, nice car and the best that money can buy — Actually, no one is telling you not to have a great house, a nice car and fine things. This principle is encouraging awareness regarding surplus hoarding and greed. It is reminding you not to overdo it with constant purchasing and amassing more than you can use. In addition to relating to excessive consumption, this principle addresses your attitude toward the things and people in your life. It encourages you not to be too attached to the great house and nice car and fine things. Enjoy them, but keep a proper perspective as to their meager importance in the larger scheme of your life.

Recently, my house in Oceanside, California, was on the alert list for evacuation as at least six devastating fires raged across the San Diego area. Some friends, living less than fifteen minutes away, had been evacuated. It was hard to breathe with the windows closed, and when we went outside, we needed to wear face scarves or masks.

As I looked at my deck and car covered with ashes and saw the dark clouds of smoke filling the sky, I pondered what I would take with me if the urgent call for immediate evacuation were to be announced. All I could think of was to take the computer hard drive with this book which I was in the process of writing, a few special photographs and pieces of jewelry.

It was a heart-opening revelation to hear everyone, from shop keepers to evacuated fire victims, sharing that their possessions did not matter as much as rescuing their neighbors. What was important was lodging, clothing and feeding the people who had been evacuated, stopping the fire's destruction and taking care of each other and the earth.

My area was not evacuated, and when I was able to open the windows, I was filled with tremendous gratitude for the fresh air that I had always taken for granted. Yes, I love fine things, but they are not as important as the non-material blessings of life.

Monkey Mind: *It's easy for you to say not to be possessive in relationships. When you are in love with someone, you are going to want to keep him or her close to you. And if you have children, you are certainly going to be attached to them!*

Reality check: Being possessive with your relationships and your children — First, I would heartily agree that when you are in love with someone, you want to keep him or her close to you. That is human nature. It is a matter of degree. When it becomes so extreme that the partner seems to be possessed or owned by you, that is the type of excess this principle cautions against.

I can recall a shift that happened for a friend who insisted on doing everything with her husband. She always wanted them to play tennis together even though he was masterful at the game and she was a beginner. It took a long time for my friend to let go of her possessiveness and send her husband off with her blessings to play tennis with his equals. When she did, she experienced a great sense of freedom and joy. My friend had not realized that she was being so possessive, and when she did notice it, she was happy to let it go.

Yes, of course you are attached to your children! You brought them into the world and are raising them. When the time comes that they start making decisions for themselves, you may be faced with challenges if you do not agree with their choices. I can recall seeing another friend's daughter dressed in a horribly clashing outfit, something like a red and blue plaid top and pink and purple polka-dot pants. I asked my friend what was up, and she confided that her daughter had started dressing herself. The child had informed her mother that she wanted to choose her own clothing, and this outfit was the result.

The good news is that the daughter was learning to think and make decisions for herself. With practice, she will probably learn to create less clashing outfits. It is much more damaging for the parent to exert heavy-handed control that crushes the child's independent spirit and destroys the opportunity for her to learn about making her own choices.

While such behavior is amusing in the early childhood stages, it becomes more challenging and possibly stressful for parents when their teenagers and adult offspring make decisions they do not support. It is wise to teach children to make good choices by providing safe opportunities for them to make appropriate decisions as they grow up. In this way, parents are teaching healthful decision-making and nurturing independence so that the children do learn to weigh decisions, develop self-control and trust themselves.

As your children become more independent, they may choose practices you do not sanction, jobs you would rather they not take, friends you definitely do not resonate with and perhaps even a mate you do not think is the right one. If they are teenagers, you can censure their behavior and do your best to win them over to your thinking. If they are adults, you risk becoming the "interfering parent." It is recommended that you always move cautiously, if at all, when expressing your opinion of what you think you know is best for them.

Actually, if you trust that you did your job of parenting well, you might be able to shift your perspective to trusting that your grown children DO know what's best for them and must have the freedom to "walk in their own moccasins." Sometimes young adults are much more expansive and global in their thinking and less restricted by the beliefs of their elders. At other times, they DO need a parent's intervention to set them straight. Both generations must learn to adapt to and negotiate with each other.

I think that a red flag that one is being possessive in any adult relationship is when you think you know more about what is good for the person than he or she knows for himself or herself. Everyone has blind spots. This is an opportunity for you to discover yours.

Monkey Mind: *I know I have too much stuff. Our closets are jammed packed. The garage shelves are overflowing, and there is almost no room to walk in the basement. I can't bear the thought of going through all of the junk I have accumulated for so many years. I don't have the time or the energy!*

Reality check: Having the time and energy to clear out surplus accumulated stuff — So often we leave excess possessions piled around in closets, attics, basements, garages and even storage units. It's a catch-22 that we don't have the energy to sort through this accumulated mass of stuff. The no-longer-wanted items take up space and exude heavy energy. They also impose memories of the past on the present moment, filling up places which could be clear and open to the new.

What does it take to sort and get rid of unneeded material possessions? It requires making the decision to do so. Once you decide that you are going to clear it all out, you have opened yourself to the possibility of getting very creative with the process. You might decide to clear one closet a week. You might hire a few teens to take everything from the garage and put it in the driveway where you can look through it. You can create piles and let your helpers pack them up.

There are a host of agencies that would be happy to pick up bags of clothing and usable items and distribute them to people who would be grateful for your unwanted possessions. You might even be able to earn money by holding a garage sale. You will be amazed how freeing and energizing it will feel to have so much clear space around you.

No-fault reflection questions for thought, discussion or journal writing

Now it's time to look at how you can apply the principle of non-hoarding or non-greed to your everyday life. Take time to think about, discuss or jot down your responses to the following questions. Remember to avoid any blame or judgment as you answer them honestly with as much detail as possible.

▲ How do you waste money and time pursuing possessions?

▲ What major items do you own that you are not using?

▲ In what ways are you living beyond your means?

▲ What items can you give away or sell?

▲ How much energy do you spend sorting, moving and storing stuff?

▲ What items, if any, have you bought to impress others?

▲ What surplus possessions do you have stored?

▲ To what particular belongings are you most attached? Why?

▲ In which relationships are you most possessive of another's energy? Why?

▲ How do you feel about the people in your life who are possessive of you? Why?

▲ Choose something or someone you are particularly attached to. What is one step you could take to let go of your possessiveness?

▲ How can you lighten up and streamline?

Now practice the Four D's to transform any disturbing thoughts

- Identify the situation that has an emotional "charge" on it
- **Distinguish** in detail what you are thinking and feeling about the upset. Experience it fully so you can let it go
- **Detach** from it. Shrink its importance. Gain distance from it
- **Dip** it in F-G-H — **Forgiveness**, **Gratitude**, and **Humor**
- **Design** a new picture with your desired outcome

Good notices list

Relax and be grateful for whatever you noticed about your own possessiveness. Remember to say "Good notice" whenever you discover something you would like to alter. Create a mental or written *Good Notices List* of the things you have noticed and are now shifting.

Potholes to avoid

▲ Stop buying more than you need

▲ Avoid being a storage pack rat

▲ Don't worry about not having enough

▲ Cease being attached to favorite possessions

▲ Stop clinging to people and things

▲ Avoid telling people what they should do

▲ Don't attempt to control or manipulate others

Tips to follow

▲ Know that the universe always provides for you

▲ Purchase and keep only what you can use

▲ Clear out possessions that you do not need
▲ Trust your relationships without trying to control them
▲ Enjoy life's finer things in moderation without hoarding
▲ Be content with less, attached to nothing
▲ Keep life simple and streamlined

From now on — Let go and relax

Take some time to review what you discovered as you explored ways you are attached to possessions and people. Sort through the thoughts and feelings that are now present in your mind and body. Allow them to be. Let go of all concerns.

Be thankful for whatever you noticed, and value the insights that came to you. Use these insights to help create any shifts you choose to make. Take a moment to trust in the natural flow of universal abundance. Actually think and feel that your efforts will be rewarded and items you need will come your way without your having to hoard possessions.

Think of yourself as an expanding consciousness. You are learning to look beyond material possessions to pursue your purpose in life. You are letting go of identifying with material things and moving into deeper spiritual development. You are learning to simplify and streamline. In doing so, you are discovering who you really are and what you have to contribute.

Let go of any reflections and thoughts of the past. Turn your attention to the present moment and the time from now on. Think about how you might integrate what you have been learning about possessiveness into your everyday life.

Sit comfortably in a quiet place and close your eyes. Forget all of your material possessions and focus within for a few moments. Go inward to find that place inside where there is peace and silence. See if you can feel contentment, safety and security in the silence within.

Take a few moments to become still and focus on your breath as it enters and leaves your body. As you inhale, breathe in this feeling of security. As you exhale, let go of everything else. You need nothing. You have everything you need now. Life's abundance continues to flow toward you.

Intention-setting and intention-achieved

As you focus on this inner stillness, ask what your intentions are regarding non-attachment. Word these intentions in positive terms as if they are happening now in the present tense. One by one, visualize and feel yourself living each intention in the present moment, having fully accomplished what you set out to achieve.

Visualize yourself allowing the people closest to you the freedom to grow in their own way. See yourself totally provided for and generous to others. Feel how satisfied you are with what you have. Enjoy the experience of being truly grateful for all of the blessings in your life. Feel yourself well taken care of, basking in the flow of universal abundance.

If you have opened up to any small degree and are willing to let go of hoarding possessions and clinging to people, you are well on your way to practicing this principle. Keep in mind these words of Paramahansa Yogananda — *"The pleasure of modern man is in getting more and more…. But isn't it better to live simply — without so many luxuries and with fewer worries? The time will come when mankind will begin to get away from the consciousness of needing so many material things. More security and peace will be found in the simple life."*[28]

Summary
Creating Social Harmony

To summarize, the first five principles are:

- Practice compassion
- Be truthful
- Respect what belongs to others
- Manage your energy
- Let go of possessiveness

Patanjali and the ancient Indian sages call these first five principles the "great, mighty, universal vows, unconditioned by place, time and class."[29] They viewed them as essential moral codes for all of humanity throughout the course of time.

When we follow these social principles, our mindfulness fosters positive interactions in all of our roles and relationships. We practice kindness, honoring all beings. We speak the truth compassionately and are true to ourselves as well as to our commitments to others. We honor everyone's possessions, relationships and accomplishments. We manage our energy, practicing moderation of sensual appetites and conscious sexuality. We do not cling to people, hoard things or take more than our share.

Living in this way, we avoid drama, conflict and confrontation and are able to create a peaceful environment at home, at work and in our community. We are mindful to avoid creating any distress for ourselves and others. Each of us does everything in our power to be a benevolent person who fosters harmony and well-being.

· Part III ·

Principles for Personal Well-Being

Introducing the Sages' Wisdom

Sometimes life is a balancing act as we juggle time schedules to take care of social commitments, our jobs, friends and family and still "make time" to take care of our own well-being. Being true to ourselves means we focus energy on our own personal development as well as on creating harmony with others.

While the first five principles address attitudes toward others that are the key to social success, the second five principles are geared to our own individual growth and well-being. These internal-development principles guide each of us to be the best person we can be. They help us to become clear on our life's purpose and to succeed at achieving it.

A look at the principles for personal well-being

In *The Secret Power of Yoga*, Nischala Joy Devi presents Patanjali's five principles for personal well-being that allow us to "journey inward toward wholeness and discovering our divinity:"

1. *"Through simplicity and continual refinement (Shaucha), the body, thoughts and emotions become clear reflections of the [joyful] Self within ...*
2. *When at peace and content with oneself and others (Santosha), supreme joy is celebrated*
3. *Living life with zeal and sincerity, the purifying flame is ignited (Tapas), revealing the inner light*
4. *Sacred study of the Divine through scripture, nature and introspection (Swadhaya) guides us to the Supreme Self*
5. *Through wholehearted dedication (Iswara Pranidhana), we become intoxicated with the Divine"* [30]

To make it simple and easy, I have captured the essence of each principle in a few words, stating it as a practice to follow:
1. Keep it clean
2. Cultivate contentment
3. Develop discipline
4. Study yourself
5. Surrender to a higher power

Let's begin exploring how you can benefit from living these personal growth principles more fully in your life starting with the practice of cleanliness.

Chapter One

Keep it Clean

~ *If you found out that someone you greatly admire was coming to visit your home, what would you have to do to get the place in order?*

~ *If you were on your deathbed and wanted to die with a pure heart, what would you need to unburden?*

~ *If you made a commitment to "clean up your life," what would you have to change?*

Pondering the answers to these three questions may arouse the need for you to practice the next principle — Keep it clean. Do you ever let things pile up until a guest comes over or let your hair go another day when you know it needs washing? Do you ever say unkind things about people without thinking or hold onto bad feelings and resentments? It is helpful to look at how you might benefit by focusing on cleaning up your mind, heart, body, speech and environment. To use a slang expression, what can you do to "clean up your act"?

The sages' wisdom

The first principle about developing ourselves to the fullest calls for cleanliness and purity in body, thought, speech and action. In pursuing this principle, we do our best to aim for a high level of cleanliness and clarity in all aspects of our lives. Aspiring to purity also entails practicing the principles of compassion, discipline and moderation. In practicing all three simultaneously, you are kind to yourself, you develop discipline for greater cleanliness and you are conscious to be moderate when you do indulge.

Obviously, on the physical level, there needs to be cleanliness of the body and both the work and home environments. Accordingly, we keep ourselves clean, bathing daily and practicing good hygiene. Maintaining a supportive environment, we keep a clean home and car, neat closets and an uncluttered office. Nurturing a healthy, energetic body, we practice conscious eating of nutritious foods. It is also recommended that we do occasional fasting or cleansing and refrain from ingesting unhealthful substances. The sages advise us to steer clear of consuming anything that may cause hyperactivity or lethargy.

On a mental level, this principle refers to keeping our minds pure, steady and free of disturbing emotions. Since the state of the body affects the mind, we need to purify the body to cultivate a peaceful mind. When the body is racing with caffeine and chocolate, the mind will tend to be quickened, and we may have restless energy.

To keep a pure mind, we do our best to release our ego thoughts and not snowball them into big issues that prevent us from being peaceful. We are mindful that life can be a roller coaster ride, so we do our best not to overindulge by carrying emotions to extreme peaks and valleys. Instead of jumping on that roller coaster ride, we stay clear when we see it coming.

A clean mind is free of hidden motives or agendas and focused on being genuinely present. Expressing a pure heart, we are forthright and clear in our actions and interactions. We are open and authentic.

Applying purity to speech, we practice being truly aware of what we say. We care how our words affect others. We are tactfully honest, and we do our best not to say damaging things or gossip about people.

The reward for purity, sages claim, is that when the body is cleansed, the mind purified and the senses subdued, we can experience the joy of our inner being. Purity, they say, brings greater clarity and receptivity to life's messages in each moment.

Now that we are no longer weighed down by heavy, emotional baggage, our attention can move inward to reflect on the profound nature of who we are deep within. Purity makes it possible for us to pursue knowing our inner spiritual nature. In refining our bodies, thoughts and emotions, we are able to access the joy within and radiate that inner spirit.

The sages assert that as we master purity, we become more astutely aware of our senses, more able to focus our attention and more clear and expansive in our perceptions. We are able to access inner joy and learn more about our higher self or core consciousness. According to Swami Satchitananda — *When we master cleanliness, we gain the purity of beingness, "cheerfulness of mind, one-pointedness, mastery over the senses, and fitness for Self-realization."*[31]

Be a self-cleaning oven

I teach my clients the concept of becoming a "self-cleaning oven." Sometimes what we are feeling is not originating within us but picked up from someone else. Just as the oven gets splashed with grease and covered with gunk, we pick up stuff that may negatively affect our energy from the people and environments we encounter.

For example, we might feel annoyed after someone has been dumping whining complaints on us and we have picked up some of that person's irritability. Or, we may spend time in a shopping mall with glaring fluorescent lights and find ourselves feeling frenzied energy that is due to that lighting.

It is good to recognize when our energy is being negatively affected and do whatever we can to clear ourselves. There are numerous ways to shift energy, such as taking a shower, applying aromatherapy oils, doing a breathing exercise, listening to soothing music, going for a walk out in nature or taking a brief time-out to sit still or lie down. If the disruption of energy Is emotional, applying the Four D's would help to Distinguish the problem, Detach from it, Dip the incident in forgiveness, gratitude and humor and Design a more appealing outcome.

While it is important not to let emotions overpower us, we do have to feel the emotions that we are experiencing just as they are without exaggerating them into greater suffering or pretending that they are less gripping than they truly are. While we do not want to add extra, long-lasting drama, we do not want to be in denial and stuff our feelings.

It is best to feel our feelings with the intention of releasing them rather than indulging ourselves in a three-week self-pity party. For example, we can remember not to get carried away with uncontrollable excitement when life gives us unexpected good fortune, and we can remind ourselves not to plunge into deep despair when something disappointing happens. Moments of joy are to be savored and disappointments are to be felt, cleared and learned from.

Practicing purity of mind, body and spirit, we do our best to stay balanced and centered through both joy and sadness, feeling our emotions and releasing them. Refraining from adding extra soap opera drama to events that happen, we aim to keep our minds clear and unclouded by distractions.

Instead of carrying the heavy baggage of accumulated past hurts, we can let go of past issues, keep our energy flowing and our hearts open. Once we know that each of us is an energy body, it becomes our job to keep on clearing that energy body and become like that self-cleaning oven.

Everyday examples

Here are a number of common examples of ways some of us may need to address greater cleanliness and purity. See if any of them apply to you.

▲ A messy car with junk on the floor and seats
▲ An office desk with too much clutter to find things
▲ A body and mind numbed by too much alcohol

- Proneness to temper tantrums instead of emotional control
- Recycling, snowballing and projecting negative emotions
- Not being able to concentrate due to problems on the mind
- Neglecting to take care of your body the way you should
- Going for periods of time without feeling peace and balance within
- Doing a favor only because you want to get something in return
- Having negative or impure thoughts about a colleague or neighbor
- Using substances or distractions to cloud the mind instead of remaining clear

"Monkey Mind" protests and reality checks

What is your Monkey Mind saying about pursuing greater cleanliness and purity in your life? See if you can relate to any of the comments noted below —

Monkey Mind: *You've got to be kidding! I can't be that pure all of the time. Sometimes I like to gorge myself on an all-you-can-eat buffet or get drunk at a happy hour with my good friends or eat that whole pint of ice cream topped with chocolate syrup and whipped cream. You can't ask me to give up everything!*

Reality check: Indulging in food and drink — Sometimes we all like to overdo it with food or beverage. The idea of following the principle of purity is to make you conscious of what you are taking into your body so that you know when you are indulging and avoid doing it too frequently. It is all about consciousness, setting standards for yourself and being moderate.

For example, I love ice cream, although I know that dairy is not healthy for me because it causes mucous build-up, and ice cream is really fattening. In the past, I used to be able to wolf down a pint of ice cream by myself without even enjoying it while I was glued to the television. Now, when I purchase ice cream, it's a big decision. At home, I take a scoop in a bowl and really savor it as a not-every-day treat. There have been times when I made the scoop a heaping one or went back for a second scoop, but I no longer ravage the whole pint! I maintain a conscious awareness that I am allowing myself to indulge, and I enjoy it. The same notion would apply to your occasional lavish dinners or happy hours. Enjoy the gourmet food, fine wine and dessert delicacies and do so consciously, in moderation. If you seriously overindulge, your body will let you know.

Monkey Mind: *You tell me to go into the stillness within. When I sit still, all I hear is my mind rambling on and on about one thing and then another. Instead of stillness, there is restlessness. I can't sit still for more than a few minutes.*

Reality check: Accessing the stillness within — The rambling you hear when you aim to quiet yourself is the Monkey Mind. Not just you, but everyone has some difficulty quieting this mental chatter. A good way to sneak up on it is to let your mind just go on and on with its stream of incessant thoughts and watch them for awhile. Give yourself some time to think of everything that is happening in your life right now. Ask yourself, "So what is on my mind these days?" Just let the thoughts float by continuously without pausing to give any of them extra attention.

In this way, you learn to become the witness to your Monkey Mind. You begin to observe it and realize that it is not who you are. You are the higher consciousness observing the monkey. You might want to do the three-part exercise outlined in Part One, Chapter II, page 25, for scanning your thoughts, emotions and body tightness to quiet your mind.

If you are a beginner at quieting your mind, please be very patient with yourself. Your Monkey Mind will always tell you that you are not doing it right. Instead of thinking that you SHOULD be able to sit in silence, think of meditation as an ongoing process of slowing down your mind a little at a time. Allow your mind to do what it does and just become its observer or witness. The first step to accessing the stillness within is to stop and observe the endless stream of rampant thoughts that run through your head. The second step is to accept that you have this restless mind and stay with the process. The third step is to watch it slow down a little, then a little more.

After a good deal of practice, you will be able to quiet the Monkey Mind, access a bit of stillness and feel some peace within. Then the process becomes more manageable. Rampant thoughts become easier to pause and put on mute. Moments of peace and stillness are reached sooner and last longer. Please have patience, continue practicing and be very compassionate with yourself.

Monkey Mind: *While I would love to have a pure heart, I cannot say that I do. There are just certain people I do not like having around. There are behaviors I do not tolerate and things I just can't stand. I guess I have my prejudices, but I am basically a good person.*

Reality check: Having judgments and intolerances — I think having a pure heart simply means being authentic and kind. It is human nature to feel more comfortable with people who are like you and less attracted to people who are unlike you. As mentioned earlier, judgment involves blame whereas discernment means making distinctions without blame. It is okay to move toward certain people you find pleasing and away from others who do not appeal to you, so long as you are not inflicting harsh blame or judgment.

The distinction of having a pure heart means that you <u>are</u> genuinely who you say you are. You are honest rather than deceptive, straightforward rather than manipulative. You practice compassion and truthfulness. You are kind to everyone and honor every person as a worthwhile being. You do not condemn people by their stereotypes without giving the individuals a chance.

Honoring all beings does not mean that you have to sanction behavior you do not tolerate. Hopefully, you can learn to summon respect for people whose conduct you disapprove of and learn to accept everyone as part of the human family.

No-fault reflection questions for thought, discussion or journal writing

Take some time to reflect upon how you might cultivate a cleaner body and environment and purify your heart and mind. The following questions suggest common ways you may choose to be more impeccable in your thoughts, speech and behavior. Think about or jot down responses to the questions below.

▲ How might you improve your personal hygiene?

▲ What aspects of your home or work environment need cleaning?

▲ In what ways might you purify your diet?

▲ What can you stop doing or start doing to create greater clarity?

▲ What is one bad habit you might plan to overcome?

▲ What thoughts do you have that are impure, negative or agenda-filled? How might you transform them?

▲ What situations do you allow to take you on an emotional roller coaster ride that disturbs your peace of mind? How can you prevent this?

▲ In what ways is your heart pure; in what ways is it not?

▲ In what ways do you honor your body as the temple of your soul?

▲ Remember a time you abused your body with overindulgence in food, alcohol, sweets or any other substance. Recall the effect it had on you.

▲ What can you do to have your body, mind and spirit in peak condition?

Now practice the Four D's to transform any disturbing thoughts

● Identify the situation that has an emotional "charge" on it

● **Distinguish** in detail what you are thinking and feeling about the upset. Experience it fully so you can let it go

● **Detach** from it. Shrink its importance. Gain distance from it

● **Dip** it in F-G-H — **Forgiveness**, **Gratitude**, and **Humor**

● **Design** a new picture with your desired outcome

Good notices list

Be thankful for whatever you discovered as you responded to these questions. Remember to practice no-fault reflection in which no blame or harsh judgment is allowed. Always take it easy on yourself. Whenever you see something you would like to shift, simply say "Good notice!" and be grateful for the awareness. Make a brief *Good Notices List* (either in your mind or on paper) of the things you have noticed and are now planning to shift regarding cleanliness and purity.

Potholes to avoid

▲ Watch that emotions don't get out of control
▲ Avoid falling behind with hygiene and cleanliness
▲ Be aware of hidden agendas behind your actions
▲ Resist distractions that cloud mental clarity
▲ Refrain from negative, judgmental thoughts
▲ Don't indulge in harmful substances
▲ Release carrying any heavy past burdens

Tips to follow

▲ Keep it light-hearted and simple
▲ Treat your body as sacred
▲ Choose a diet that's good for you
▲ Cultivate a clean environment
▲ Let go of emotional drama and trauma
▲ Keep your mind clear and present
▲ Take time to experience the stillness within

From now on — Let go and relax

Relax your mind for a few moments. Let go of any thoughts prompted by the reflection questions. Take a deep breath and exhale with a sigh, releasing any emotions that thoughts may have aroused. Think about what you realized as you answered these questions. What Earth School lessons have these past experiences taught you? How can you bring greater cleanliness into your life in little ways on a daily basis? Remember to be compassionate with yourself and take small steps when you see ways to bring about desired changes.

Sit comfortably, away from any distractions, and close your eyes. Take a few moments to become as still as you can in this moment. Take a deep belly breath and exhale with an audible sigh. Do this a few times to release emotions and toxins. Then simply follow your breath as it enters through the tips of your nostrils. As you inhale, focus on your clarity and the purity of your spirit in the present moment. As you exhale, let go of everything you are holding from the past. Repeat inhaling the present clarity and exhaling the past several times until your mind and body become quiet. Enjoy the moments of stillness and silence.

Intention-setting and intention-achieved

From this peaceful place, think about how you can purify your body to access the spirit within. Ask yourself what you intend to do to "clean up" your life. What practices will help you become clearer and more attuned to your inner being? Think for a while. Then see what intentions come to mind. Jot down your intentions, posing them in positive statements in the present tense as if you are already experiencing them.

Take time with each intention so that you can see and feel yourself living it fully. Then slowly move on to intensely experience your other intentions, one at a time. Visualize yourself happily enjoying a sparkling clean environment. Experience yourself having a perfectly healthy body and consciously choosing foods that are good for you. See yourself radiating a light-hearted purity and well-being.

Ponder these words from BKS Iyengar — *"When the body is cleansed, the mind purified, and the senses controlled, joyful awareness needed to realize the inner self, also comes. With cleanliness, the body becomes the temple of the seer and feels the joy of self awareness. When the consciousness is cheerful and benevolent, the seeker becomes ready to receive the knowledge and vision of the soul."*[32]

Chapter Two

Cultivate Contentment

Imagine what it would be like if you could take a jar of copper pennies and magically turn them into gold coins. With the price of gold today, you could be an instant millionaire! Wouldn't it be great to be an alchemist?!

In medieval times, an alchemist was a person who practiced the chemistry of turning base metals into gold. I am sure you will agree that this is a wonderful concept for enriching abundance. You, too, can become an alchemist.

You can learn to practice your own form of alchemy as you turn life's less-than-grand moments into valuable experiences. No matter what happens in life, all circumstances are transitory and seen through each individual's subjective viewpoint. Nothing is by nature "negative." The negativity exists only in our perceptions. Since all perceptions are created by us, why not mine for gold and turn unappreciated occurrences into golden moments?

As alchemists, we can also reach for the "silver lining" and possible benefits in everything that occurs. In Earth School, everything that happens is here to teach us and is beneficial in that respect. Every moment we have lived has unfolded just right. It is all perfect in the scheme of our lives. All events lead to new decisions and new directions. We can learn to turn the pennies of life into solid gold just by shifting our awareness.

The sages' wisdom

The second personal development principle is to cultivate contentment and good-heartedness. The sages urge us to be willing to accept whatever fate may bring us with balance, gratitude and joy. They encourage us to detach from our daily experience and become objective witnesses, observing ourselves on a transcendent level. They urge us to be impartial spectators, sitting in the stands, viewing ourselves playing out our lives on the stage. As witnesses, we are not attached to particular outcomes. We learn to be satisfied with whatever may happen.

Practicing contentment does not mean that we never experience dis-satisfaction with circumstances. As the proverbial saying goes, "When life gives us lemons, we make lemonade." We are simply willing to make the most of any situation. It does not guarantee that we will never get frustrated or emotionally upset. When life does throw us off center, aligning with our commitment to be content helps us focus on the good and get right back into balance. In addition to applying this contentment to our own lives, we express a good-heartedness and benevolence to others as well, allowing people to be as they are without judgment.

It is helpful to develop a constant awareness and vigilance over judging, which is one of the Monkey Mind's favorite pastimes. Saying "Good notice!" and shifting from judging to kindness is a great practice to develop as we pursue becoming more compassionate.

The sages say that by practicing contentment and good-heartedness, we can attain supreme happiness.[33] No matter what happens, we can bring satisfaction to life by expressing our gratitude. We can dwell on appreciating what we have instead of lamenting what we do not have. Focusing on our inner being, we can identify more with the core essence of who we are than with experiences outside of us.

When we are feeling out of harmony with life, we can practice contentment by taking steps to center ourselves and become satisfied with what is. We can be grateful that what is happening points to the need for change. When challenging things happen, we must accept them before anything can lighten up. In severely troubling times, we may need to seek professional help.

Sages teach us that suffering is the pain we add when we do not like what is happening. As such, they are pointing out that suffering is a matter of choice. While we do have to experience some pain or grief as the wheel of life rolls around, we do not have to create additional misery by magnifying negativity and adding emotional trauma.

In the ultimate practice of contentment, we maintain unwavering serenity in the presence of life's ups and downs. Practicing alchemy, we can acknowledge the value of life's disappointments as Earth School lessons. We can learn to view the apparent "breakdowns" as messages from the universe that a needed "breakthrough" is at hand. Through eyes of unconditional love, we can see pain and pleasure, hardship and ease, without succumbing to emotional disturbance. The sages propose that when we master contentment, we will be supremely happy and totally free of desires and attachments.

Turn issues into blessings

Instead of turning perceptions into issues, we can choose to turn them into blessings. We can simply let go of any negativity and focus on being grateful. We can avoid turning ourselves into victims, like the wife who still complains about the husband who left her ten years ago. No matter what happens, we can do our best to maintain emotional serenity. If we get caught in the emotions, we can free ourselves from them as soon as possible and return to a peaceful state. We can remember to trust in the flow of events and have faith that everything that happens is somehow ultimately for the highest good.

Sometimes, a person is fired from a job because there is a more rewarding one coming. Someone may lose a partner because there is one who is a more perfect match about to show up. We might miss a train because we are supposed to meet someone. If we review our life experience, we will probably think of several events that seemed negative at the time but later presented opportunities.

Seeing the blessings comes after feeling the initial emotions and allowing them to be there. As you know, it is not healthy to stuff or deny emotions and cover them up with positive thinking. A rather crude metaphor for this would be "putting on perfume to cover up body odor." It just does not work! It is always beneficial to feel our genuine emotions so that we can release them. Then from a place of peace and clarity, we can ask the question, "Why is this happening?" Perhaps some insights will occur to us if we do not get caught in the drama.

Contentment is achieved one decision at a time

Contentment is achieved one decision at a time. We decide to be good-natured when we wake up in the morning. We make a commitment to be satisfied with whatever our day might bring.

As mentioned in the Author's Preface, I, personally, am not a smiling, Sally Sunshine type of person. Yet, in my heart, I am truly grateful for every part of my life. However, I do have to watch out for pot holes that I can so easily step into. Each day I pray that I may respond to whatever life sends me with grace and ease. Some days I experience more grace and ease than others, but it is always my goal. In this way, I cultivate contentment on a daily basis.

I have come to realize that being content means being "in accord" or "okay" with whatever happens — as in surrendering our likes and dislikes to achieving harmony with ourselves and others in life.

I can recall tossing about unable to sleep with a noisy group of drinkers partying in the campsite adjacent to mine. I lay awake, saying to myself — "I can be okay with this." After a while, I did not even hear them. Before learning to put harmony first, I might have gotten angry at the noisy campers or gotten up to ask them to be quiet. Instead, I just allowed and let myself take a moment to be okay with it. You might use the Four D's when you fall out of accord with events to harmonize yourself with whatever pulled you off center.

When you make a commitment to be content, you are deciding to be both good-natured and in harmony with everyone and everything. That does not mean you agree with everything or everyone, but that you are able to recognize what is happening and align your energy to be okay with it for the time being. You can reap the value of the messages that everything brings, especially what they teach you about yourself. Instead of seeing the proverbial "half-empty glass," you can intend to focus on the "half-full glass." You can become the alchemist who can transform the worst situation into a glorious celebration!

Everyday examples

Here are several examples of ways people tend to be less than content with life. See if any of them apply to you.

▲ Complaining about your lot in life
▲ Telling the same bad experience to bunches of people
▲ Thinking — "When am I ever going to get a break?!"
▲ Focusing on what you do not have instead of what you have
▲ Being unhappy with yourself for things you have or haven't done
▲ Wishing you were in someone else's shoes
▲ Carrying longtime grudges and resentments
▲ Feeling unlucky at love or cards or anything
▲ Thinking that if one thing happened, then you would be happy
▲ Blaming others in your life for your discontent
▲ Not trusting that life's flow of abundance will reach you

"Monkey Mind" protests and reality checks

You may find your mind automatically spouting responses similar to those that follow. What is your Monkey Mind saying about being content? See if any of the following thoughts relate to you —

Monkey Mind: *You make it sound so easy to accept whatever* *happens. Suppose you suddenly lose your job. You are laid off from a ten-year job due to down-sizing. Now you cannot afford to pay the rent or bills. How can you be grateful for that?!*

Reality check: Accepting harsh circumstances and remaining grateful — It is certainly a jolt to lose your job after ten years of service. I do not think anyone in this situation would slip instantly into gratitude. There is a step to take before looking for the benefits to the situation. That step is accepting the way it is and acknowledging the way you feel. You have to give yourself the space to feel whatever is there for you.

Rather than magnify the negative aspects and snowball your upset into a drama of chronic proportions, you can allow yourself to be hurt and feel the emotions. Feel the disappointment and see if you can somehow diminish or release the emotions; then look beyond them. Do your best to accept the situation, detach from it and create a shift. You can practice the Four D's.

Getting emotionally upset, complaining about the boss and making yourself feel like a poor, abused victim is not going to help you find another job and take care of your family. It is the drama you add that makes disappointments more self-abusive than they really are. While you may feel some pain upon losing a job, you do not need to add more suffering to the situation. Eventually, when you have recovered from the shock, you might see some new possibilities and be grateful for the turn of events.

Monkey Mind: *There are a lot of things I yearn to have in my life, a lot of things missing. How can I be content with the way things are when I know I need and deserve more?*

Reality check: Yearning for more and being content — As long as you keep lamenting what's missing, you will continue to experience what's missing. What you think is what you get. Being content with the way it is does not mean you are not intending to have your dreams unfold.

When you repeat complaints, it is as if you are sending out a negative mantra, asking the universe to send you more of the same. It is as if you are decreeing the lamentable situation to remain in existence when you complain that — "Life is not good to me... Life is not good to me... Life is not good to me." Or, perhaps your lament is calling for scarcity to continue — "I don't have enough money...I don't have enough money...I don't have enough money!" Dwelling on such dissatisfaction and repeatedly expressing it will only bring you more of the same — life's not being good to you and your not having enough money.

Being content simply means being wise enough to accept the way life is for you right now and looking at ways to be satisfied with what you have. At the same time, you are being temporarily satisfied with current circumstances, you are planning to have your desires fulfilled and holding on to a vivid vision of having what you want. You can apply the Four D's discussed earlier by Distinguishing what you are dissatisfied with and Detaching from making it seem so dramatic. Then do the triple Dip. Decide what you can forgive, what you can be grateful for and what you can find humorous in your circumstances. Lastly, Design what you want, holding firmly to your intention, and visualize it happening.

Monkey Mind: *It is easy to shift to accepting what happens when it's something little. But you can't pull a miraculous "gratitude shift" when something catastrophic happens like the discovery of chronic cancer or the unexpected death of a loved one.*

Reality check: Shifting to gratitude amid catastrophic circumstances — I totally agree that it is not easy to shift into gratitude when something catastrophic happens. Yet, you will see cancer patients, even those at stage four, accepting what they cannot change because there is nothing else to do but accept it and do their best to heal. Discovering that you have an illness can catapult you into appreciating each and every moment of life to the extent of savoring the time you have left. Sometimes when life gives you what you do not want, it helps you clarify what you do want.

I remember when my mother had a stroke and was both paralyzed and speech impaired. The only sound she could mouth came out sounding like a tormented "Why...why...why?" She was unable to be rehabilitated and remained institutionalized. My father visited her every night, bringing soft food to feed her and the clothing he had taken home to wash from the night before. Everyone in our family was utterly distraught. For my father, *the gratitude was that she was still there. His wife was still alive.*

Her plight became worse when one of the staff reported that she had developed gangrene in her foot. They wanted to amputate her leg. My father said he could not give permission for them to cut off my mother's leg and then have to tell her the next day. So he took her out of the home to see a doctor he knew, pleading for help. This doctor was able to amputate only the front half of mother's foot, leaving a stump of a heel, much like a deer's foot. *Our whole family felt truly grateful that the doctor had saved Mom's leg and just amputated part of her foot.*

When Mom died several months later, my sisters, brother and I were all grief-stricken to no longer have our mother as was our father to lose his wife. Yet, somehow, *we were grateful that she was out of her misery.*

And as my mother lay in her coffin at a wake for three days, *I sat with different family members and asked what they loved most about Mom, infusing the room with a quality of gratitude.* They said things like "Margie was Christmas!" and "Margie could kick a football three blocks with her bare foot." I included each comment in a moving eulogy that had everyone present tearful as we celebrated Mom's life. You might remember to do this when a loved one passes.

No matter how catastrophic the circumstances, the only thing that works is to stay in the now and make the best of the present moment. You have to feel what you feel, which may involve some grieving. You can be gentle with yourself, take some time to grieve and be satisfied with the fact that what there is for you to do now is to grieve. Meanwhile, you can continue to find satisfaction and be grateful for each of life's blessings. That is all there is to do.

No-fault reflection questions for thought, discussion or journal writing

Take some time to reflect upon how you might cultivate greater contentment in your daily life. The following reflection questions invite you to look at specific areas in which you might apply your own personal form of alchemy to transform your responses to challenging situations. Think about, discuss or jot down responses to your choice of the questions below.

▲ What occurrences in your life tend to get you hooked or emotionally disturbed?

▲ What strategies do you use to catch yourself before reacting negatively?

▲ Think of a time you got upset over negative circumstances and review the outcome. How could you have responded more appropriately?

▲ Recall a time when you were able to remain centered in the midst of challenging circumstances. What did you do, and how did you feel?

▲ What percentage of the time are you content with yourself and your life? What undermines your contentment the remainder of the time?

▲ What do you generally do to overcome feeling distressed by troubling circumstances?

▲ In what ways are you satisfied with your life and in what ways are you dissatisfied with it? What would need to shift for you to be satisfied with your life all of the time?

▲ If life presents a series of ups and downs, how can you manage to keep yourself content every day of your life?

▲ Think about some of the worst things that have happened in your life and how you survived them.

▲ Recall telling several people about a troubling incident. How did it make you feel to repeat it, and how do you think it made them feel to hear it?

▲ Begin an ongoing list of reasons to be grateful. Every day, think of at least three new reasons to be grateful.

Now Practice the Four D's
to transform any disturbing thoughts

- Identify the situation that has an emotional "charge" on it
- **Distinguish** in detail what you are thinking and feeling about the upset. Experience it fully so you can let it go
- **Detach** from it. Shrink its importance. Gain distance from it
- **Dip** it in F-G-H — **Forgiveness**, **Gratitude**, and **Humor**
- **Design** a new picture with your desired outcome

Good notices list

Take a few moments to be grateful now. Be thankful for the insights that came from these questions. Remember not to be harsh with yourself when you see something you would like to shift. Simply acknowledge yourself for noticing it. Say "Good notice!" Make a brief *Good Notices List* (either mental or written) of the things you are now planning to shift to create greater contentment in your life.

Potholes to avoid

▲ Avoid taking negative circumstances to heart

▲ Refrain from re-running troubling incidents

▲ Don't view yourself as a helpless victim

▲ Remember not to carry past burdens forward

▲ Stop snowballing little troubles into big ones

▲ Shift your focus away from scarcity or loss

▲ Don't let others drag you down

Tips to follow

▲ Be content with who you are as you are

▲ Shift to being satisfied with whatever life brings

▲ Accept what is so and what is not

▲ Live from a place of satisfaction and joy

▲ See God's goodness everywhere

▲ Rejoice in the flow of life

▲ Be grateful for everything that happens

From now on — Let go and relax

Now it is time to relax and let go of any feelings the questions may have prompted. Focus on ways to bring more contentment to your everyday life. As a student in Earth School, you are learning quickly. Think about what you discovered as you pondered the questions. Based on your insights, what shifts would you like to bring about? Explore your intentions for increasing contentment. How can you bring greater satisfaction to your everyday life and experience more gratitude?

Sit still in a comfortable place. Close your eyes and focus on your breathing. Take in a deep breath. Hold that breath for a few seconds and then exhale very slowly, and hold your breath out for a few moments. Repeat this breathing in and holding, then breathing out more slowly and holding the breath out for a few seconds until you are able to quiet your mind and focus your attention inward. Then return to breathing naturally, with your eyes closed, nestling into that peaceful place of silence within.

Intention-setting and intention-achieved

Think about what you intend to do and create intentions for being content from now on. Start to visualize yourself achieving each intention, one at a time. Summon the faces of any people involved. See and feel yourself living each intention in succession, experiencing great contentment with each person. Experience what it is like for you to be truly satisfied with your life and all the people in it. Feel yourself radiating love from a content heart. Take a few moments to become as still as you can in this moment. Focus on feeling contentment inside. See how many reasons you have to smile, and feel your joy.

If you have thought of at least a few ways that you can make yourself more content with the circumstances and people in your life, you are successfully applying this principle of contentment. As you focus on living a life of contentment, remember these words from Swami Satchidananda — *"As a result of contentment, one gains supreme joy…. Contentment means just to be as we are without going to outside things for our happiness. If something comes, we let it come. If not, it doesn't matter."*[34]

Chapter Three

Develop Discipline

What pictures does the word "discipline" evoke in your mind's eye? Does it conjure images of helpless, teary-eyed youngsters with their hands being smacked hard by a school master's ruler or their buttocks being whipped to redness by an angry father's belt strap? Sadly, for many people, the word "discipline" may evoke images of punishing others or being punished by them. It may arouse painful memories of being chastised for things they did or did not do.

In contrast, your pictures of "discipline" may have conjured images of the list of things you have wanted the power to achieve. Perhaps you saw yourself having the strength to lose that excess ten pounds or to stick to that exercise routine or to actually read the many books you have accumulated.

For some, the word "discipline" may summon pictures of military rigor or the discipline that trainers require of athletes and ballerinas to achieve success. Sometimes the discipline structure from the outside is agreed upon as part of entering an educational program, adopting a volunteer role in the community or accepting a job at work.

In most cases, the structure of discipline imposed from the outside has to be met with internal discipline to fulfill requirements and expectations. It helps to remember to summon the discipline needed to make life run smoothly. For example, if the imposed speed limit is 65 mph, we need to have the discipline to adhere to that or possibly suffer consequences.

Take at look at the facets of discipline operating in your life. Notice instances in which you must follow the discipline imposed by authorities at work, at home or in society as well as situations that require that you exert your own self-discipline. What do you notice?

Discipline as self-love

Discipline has gotten "a bad rap"! It has the connotation of an authority figure chastising us or doing whatever it takes to whip us into shape. *There is a great difference between discipline inflicted on us from the outside, which can be a form of control, punishment or manipulation, and discipline from the inside, which is a form of nurturing self-love.*

In reality, self-discipline is a good thing. It's about doing what is needed to bring out our best. Having discipline means we are "compassionately rigorous" with ourselves. In a wholesome way, we push ourselves to achieve our goals and do what is beneficial for our bodies, minds, spirits and all of our roles and relationships.

We are treating ourselves well when we develop discipline over the many distractions that can pull us away from accomplishing our goals. Practicing discipline helps us achieve a type of mental strength and control over our bodies, minds and speech. Being disciplined is a way of loving ourselves and bringing out our best. We are rigorous with ourselves because we care about the life we are creating and how we show up in the world.

The sages' wisdom

From the principles of purity and contentment, we move to a more deeply profound concept — developing discipline. According to the sages, we burn away any impurities through strict self-discipline in three areas: the body, mind and speech.

For example, to discipline the body, we might fast to cleanse our digestive system and organs, stay on a healthy food regimen and exercise to burn calories. To discipline the mind, we might let go of memories of past hurts and stop thinking negative thoughts about things lacking in our lives. We might remember to shift from judging to accepting people as they are. Lastly, to discipline speech, we might be mindful not to say anything offensive, to tailor our speech to be consistently kind and to avoid engaging in gossip. We could also develop self-discipline to resist distractions, hone skills and perform tasks required to excel in our careers.

The ancient sages speak of this principle as "burning away" or removing whatever does not serve your well-being. They recommend developing the austerity or rigorous performance that overcomes the pull of desires. The practice of discipline entails endurance, will-power and character building.

The sages' wisdom is to develop the discipline to burn away all impurities and eliminate desires that get in the way of achieving goals. Mastering discipline brings about many rewards. The sages claim that having the discipline to purge impurities helps us refine our inner being and access our full potential and greatest power.[35]

Discipline with compassion

While applying self-discipline, we must also practice compassion, the paramount principle. Discipline must never be brutal or hurtful but always tempered with loving kindness.

Take, for example, an advertising executive who is spending the whole weekend working on a very important presentation for her company's biggest client on Monday. While she is driven to get it done and have it be excellent, she needs to also be kind to herself in the process.

Although spending most of the day riveted to the computer, she can refresh herself by taking breaks and perhaps go out in nature for a walk. She can stop to enjoy her favorite foods and make sure that she has enough sleep as she keeps working at completing her project throughout the weekend. During the whole time, her intense focus is on creating an excellent presentation, so she practices discipline to keep away from activities that might distract her such as lengthy telephone conversations or television movies. In this way, she is practicing both discipline and compassion for herself.

Discipline, defined as "burning impurities" by the sages, entails eliminating whatever might interfere with accomplishing the goal. Although discipline suggests an intense rigor, the message is an uplifting one. Having discipline to do what needs to be done is being compassionate to ourselves. The idea is to develop greater zeal in keeping the promises we make to ourselves for our own benefit and the welfare of others.

To summon this zeal, we need to access a place of inner strength, endurance and will power. Discipline can be viewed as "tough love" or being "fierce" with ourselves to achieve what is beneficial. Being fierce with ourselves means keeping our word to do what we said we would do.

Have you noticed that the promises people tend to break most easily are the ones they make to themselves? Being fierce means saying — "That's it! I am quitting this now, or I am starting this now — no doubt about it, no ands, ifs or buts! This ends now! That starts now!"

Being fierce with ourselves about the important things is like strong parenting. It entails emphatic resolve on our part to transcend any and all temptation to backslide and actually mean it this time. Being fierce with ourselves can help us overcome the tendency to hold promises to ourselves lightly.

We need to be fierce as in "really meaning it," but never harsh. And if backsliding happens, we must be compassionate. We might fall short once or twice before we can exert our full willpower. Once we really make a commitment to our well-being, the promises we make to nurture ourselves will be the most important ones.

Know that by practicing discipline, you become "a crusader for your own well-being." I invite you to use this principle to reflect upon any current situations in your life that may require greater discipline and examine your efforts to achieve your most passionate goals.

Let's refrain from whipping ourselves with "Shoulds and Shouldn'ts"

As part of our human conditioning, we often tend to perpetuate the punishing aspect of discipline mentioned earlier. When we go ahead and do something that we lack the discipline to stop, often we may apply the whip of self-criticism. For example, a man gives in to having a cigarette when he says he wants to stop smoking. Instead of enjoying that cigarette, he feels bad while smoking it because he is thinking that he shouldn't be smoking.

Or perhaps it's a second piece of chocolate cake or a syrupy banana split that is a woman's breach of discipline. Instead of savoring the sugary treats, she feels guilty and beats herself up with "shoulds and shouldn'ts" before, during and after the brief moment of indulging in sweets. Sometimes we are able to be self-disciplined and at other times we may backslide a bit. The important thing to remember is to always be kind to ourselves and enjoy what we decide to do. Consciously choosing moderation is also a form of discipline.

Another instance of this punishing type of discipline is when we have something that we must do but are not doing. Often we chastise ourselves with the idea that it needs to be done and we should be doing it. For example, I have a small black and white tile kitchen floor that shows every tiny spot. I sometimes look at it as I leave the house and say, "I should wash that kitchen floor" and feel bad about it for a few seconds. But, if I have an important meeting that I don't want to be late for, I remember to be compassionate with myself and make a mental note to take care of it as soon as I return. In reality, it takes less than ten minutes to wash this little floor area. I am reminded of the Nike slogan — "Just do it!"

There's a colloquial expression — "When you're hot, you're hot, and when you're not, you're not." Well, the same goes for this principle — "When you are disciplined, you're disciplined, and when you're not, you're not." *Let us all beware of beating ourselves up with "shoulds and shouldn'ts" and allow ourselves to be human while holding high standards for our behavior.*

Everyday examples

The following are examples of the need for self-discipline in mind, body and speech. See if you can relate to any of them.

▲ Going off your diet plan

▲ Letting loose a tirade against someone

▲ Being mentally distracted from what you're doing

▲ Missing a few days of your exercise regimen

▲ Being unable to overcome past resentments

▲ Attending a meeting without being fully prepared

▲ Accidentally saying insensitive things

▲ Not being able to focus your mind on the goal

▲ Not getting ready in time and being late

▲ Operating at 75% of your usual capacity

▲ Leaning on others to do your job

"Monkey Mind" protests and reality checks

What is your Monkey Mind saying about practicing greater discipline in your thoughts, speech and actions? See if any of the following remarks might apply to you —

Monkey Mind: *It's not so easy to watch what you say. Sometimes I get pulled into a heated argument and have to attack the other person to defend myself. It happens in an instant before I can avoid it.*

Reality check: Getting swept into heated arguments — Yes, you can find yourself swept into a heated argument, and it can be very frustrating when someone is confronting you. Nevertheless, you can discipline yourself not to verbally attack anyone. This is a perfect time for you to move away from the person arguing. Back off in any way possible, even if it means taking a moment to leave the room. Or, say that you are not going to have the discussion at this time but will talk matters over calmly later. "Bite the bullet" if you have to. Whatever technique you use, find a way to disengage. Keep your commitment to discipline your speech. This way you will avoid saying anything you have to regret and apologize for later.

Monkey Mind: *I already know what my bad habits are. I quit smoking regularly. Then something happens to trigger the craving, and my self-discipline is not strong enough. What can I do!?*

Reality check: Having self-discipline to quit bad habits — Yes, I know how hard it is to quit smoking and then something triggers a need to have a cigarette. This plight was made humorous by Mark Twain, who wrote — *"Giving up smoking is the easiest thing in the world. I know because I've done it thousands of times."* You have to simply practice truthfulness and compassion for yourself along with practicing discipline. The ten ancient principles are all practiced simultaneously, and practicing compassion is paramount.

Perhaps the truth is that you are not ready to stop smoking yet. Maybe quitting "cold-turkey" is too drastic a move at this time. You may need to be more gentle with yourself and slowly wean yourself off smoking. You could allow yourself one cigarette a day. If you have been smoking a pack a day mindlessly, start being mindful of when you reach for a cigarette and why. Reducing a bad habit is a way of whittling it down until you can let go of it altogether. Always have compassion for yourself while practicing discipline.

Monkey Mind: *I try to keep pure thoughts, but I find myself automatically making judgments about people. I watch what they do and do not do, and I cannot help but have opinions about them in my mind.*

Reality check: Having pure thoughts vs. judging people — You really cannot control the thoughts that run rampant through your Monkey Mind. They just flow in automatically and unconsciously. However, once you become conscious of a negative thought about someone or a judgment, you can say *"Good notice!"* and shift to letting that thought go rather than making it worse or fixing it permanently in stone. Instead, you can take time to consider the person's point of view and see if you can empathize. You can look to find a more positive way to view that individual.

If the person is doing something you abhor, you can still object to the behavior without condemning the person with blame. For example, if someone is talking foolishly without thinking, you can dislike the way he is speaking, but instead of chalking him off as "an idiot," you can still honor him as a person you don't quite agree with.

While you cannot totally control what passes through your thoughts, you can control what stays and what gets dismissed. It is a matter of developing discipline or mindfulness to monitor your thoughts. Choose the ones to keep and the ones to let go. In this way, you practice compassion and increase control over your Monkey Mind.

No-fault reflection questions for thought, discussion or journal writing

Now turn your attention toward your own practice of discipline. Look at ways you are already quite disciplined and ways you could develop greater discipline of your body, mind and speech. Review the following questions, and see what responses they evoke.

▲ What is one unhealthy habit you need greater discipline to overcome? How might you achieve that?

▲ What efforts have you made to discipline bodily desires?

▲ Recall one challenging situation in which you were careful about what you said and another in which you were careless and regretted your words. Compare the outcomes.

▲ What is one current area in which you need to apply greater discipline to achieve a goal?

▲ Think of an incident in which you were able to summon self-discipline to endure hardship. What was the outcome?

▲ What project or goal calls to you with a burning desire in this moment? What steps might you take to begin it?

▲ In what areas of your life could you practice being more fierce with yourself?

▲ Describe one important goal in your life for which you are willing to overcome distractions and stay steadfast through challenges.

▲ In what ways might you benefit from greater discipline in your speaking?

▲ In what ways could you practice more self-discipline over your thoughts?

▲ How might you surrender to more fully accept the discipline imposed by authorities?

Now practice the Four D's to transform any disturbing thoughts

- Identify the situation that has an emotional "charge" on it
- **Distinguish** in detail what you are thinking and feeling about the upset. Experience it fully so you can let it go
- **Detach** from it. Shrink its importance. Gain distance from it
- **Dip** it in F-G-H — **Forgiveness**, **Gratitude**, and **Humor**
- **Design** a new picture with your desired outcome

Good notices list

Step back from these questions a moment and relax with whatever came up for you regarding discipline. Be grateful for the discoveries that opened up for you. Be kind to yourself and others about anything you would like to shift. Acknowledge yourself for your new awareness and willingness to shift. Congratulate yourself, saying — "Good notice!" Make a brief, mental or written *Good Notices List* of the things you are now planning to shift to summon more self-discipline in your life.

Potholes to avoid

▲ Stop your mind from rambling needlessly

▲ Be mindful not to speak without thinking

▲ Avoid wasting energy needed for your goals

▲ Prevent others from distracting your focus

▲ Avoid delaying attention to projects

▲ Do not lose sight of your intentions

▲ Notice when your willpower weakens

Tips to follow

▲ Learn to keep promises made to yourself

▲ Honor the discipline imposed by authority

▲ Be in charge of the thoughts you think

▲ Be mindful of the language and tone you use

▲ Do whatever is appropriate to achieve your goals

▲ Learn to quickly unplug from distractions

▲ Give each task your 100% effort

From now on — Let go and relax

Now it's time to return to the present moment, release thoughts of the past and explore ways to develop discipline from now on. Think about what you discovered as you pondered the reflection questions and the shifts you would like to bring about. Where in your life would you like to have greater zeal with yourself in accomplishing your goals? What practices would you like to institute or abandon in your life? What steps can you take to strengthen your resolve?

Make yourself comfortable in a seated position and close your eyes. Take a deep breath, inhaling the strength to have greater self-discipline. Exhale, letting go of any doubts or fears you might have about not succeeding. Repeat inhaling strength and exhaling doubt as you deepen your breathing and let go of thinking altogether.

Focus on your natural breathing pattern. Observe your breath as it comes in through your nostrils, expands your belly and then exits through your nostrils as your belly relaxes. Taking deep breaths that expand the belly, then lifting the diaphragm and exhaling fully is another technique for relaxing the body. Focus on your breath in this way for a while until you feel yourself really letting go of doubts or fears and summoning new strength and self-discipline.

Intention-setting and intention-achieved

Start composing your intentions for increasing self-discipline from now on. Once you are pleased with the wording of each intention, begin to visualize it in effect. See yourself having the discipline to accomplish one intention at a time and feel the benefits of succeeding.

Visualize the positive results of your actions as you see yourself masterfully accomplishing whatever you intended. Focus on enjoying this feeling of having the discipline to overcome unwanted habits and achieve all of your goals.

As you make a commitment to be more disciplined, remember to always be gentle with yourself at the same time that you are zealously working to attain your goals. Take small, achievable steps and congratulate yourself on each success along the way to 100% accomplishment. Always be compassionate to forgive yourself when lapses occur and then renew your commitment.

If you are able to diminish unwanted habits and increase self-nurturing activities to any small degree, you are to be acknowledged for practicing greater discipline. Keep in mind that developing discipline is a way of being kind and compassionate to yourself and others. Remember the words of author Jim Rohn — *"Discipline is the bridge between goals and accomplishment"* and the wisdom of President Theodore Roosevelt — *"With self-discipline most anything is possible."*

Chapter Four

Study Yourself

*"The more effective our study,
the more we understand our weaknesses and strengths.
We learn to nullify our weaknesses
and use our strengths to the maximum.
Then, there is no limit to our understanding."*[36]

How well do you know your own strengths and weaknesses? Take a few moments to ask yourself, first — "What are my strengths?" Then take time to reflect upon — "What are my weaknesses?" You might even draw a line down the middle of a paper and list your strengths on one side and weaknesses on the other.

How well do you know yourself? And how are you using your strengths to overcome your weaknesses?

The fourth personal growth principle advocates ongoing reflection and self-study to maximize your strengths. Whenever you make self-assessments, always inquire without allowing any blame or harsh judgment. Be grateful for whatever you notice.

The sages' wisdom

This principle teaches us to develop our best selves and discover our life purpose. Sages recommend that we access our highest being through ongoing reflection, worthwhile reading, consciousness-raising gatherings and spiritual practice. These actions, they suggest, will lead us to communion with our core goodness and universal oneness.

In ancient times, this principle alluded to reading sacred scriptures and gathering in "satsangas" or "meetings in truth" intended to raise consciousness. Today it can be broadened to include expanding self-awareness through uplifting reading, gatherings and spiritual practice. The sages teach that the reward of ongoing self-study is that it brings us closer and closer to knowing the divine source of all that is.[37]

Applying this principle of contemplative self-study, we can learn to practice constant awareness that is free of blame. We can become the non-judgmental, discerning witnesses of our own actions. Learning to reflect upon our own moment-to-moment behavior, we can use the ten principles in this book as our standards and shift to practicing them whenever we veer off course.

As we develop greater awareness, we can learn to monitor our own thoughts, actions and speech throughout each day. Rather than have a fixed worldview, we can remain open to reflection and change. While performing our various day-to-day roles, we can take time to review how well we are connecting with other people. We can keep our hearts open and engage in life experiences to heighten our consciousness.

Pursuing reading and activities that help you grow

For this principle of self-study, I like to use the metaphor of each person being a sacred chalice — a beautiful, golden jeweled chalice like those belonging to the medieval knights. Perhaps we can all think of ourselves as empty chalices to be filled with whatever we choose to put inside us. Moment-to-moment, we can be aware of how we are filling our chalices. As we monitor our intake of life experiences, we can choose activities that will enhance our aliveness and learn to recognize and release those which may be harmful to us or even toxic. Take a moment to think about what you are filling your chalice with these days.

Pursuing the highest, clearest, brightest energy we can find, we participate with others in meaningful events or entertainment and engage in worthwhile reading. We can take time to read works by master thinkers and experts on a variety of topics either in print or online.

The principle of self-study encourages us to join group activities so that we can learn from being with others who are focused on personal growth. We can choose to attend whatever church, synagogue or spiritual service we are called to, but participation does not have to be religious in nature.

We can participate in agencies that contribute to the community such as Habitat for Humanity or the Humane Society. We can join any group that encourages positive values and healthy participation, such as the company's athletic team, the Elks, the Knights of Columbus, our local Chamber of Commerce or the neighborhood senior citizens' group.

Following career interests, we can join professional groups and attend their functions to grow in knowledge in our fields of interest. Volunteering to work at the library, participating in a writing group, or attending a meditation class— all are ways of engaging in positive interaction with others. The idea is to participate in new experiences that can promote our personal development and expansion and make us feel good about ourselves, other people and life in general.

Studying ourselves entails taking time to go inward more often and developing the ability to access and clear our inner feelings. We can slow down, become more aware and reflect on how we are treating ourselves and others. We can pause often to look at how we are living our lives.

Expanding consciousness through prayer and mantra

Ultimately, true self-study entails going deeper within to discover and feel our connectedness with all that is, our oneness with the divine energy of which we are all a part. This principle calls to us to still the Monkey Mind and find that sacred inner peace that we all have within. It calls us to focus on a higher power and deepen our devotion in prayer or mantra in whatever way is comfortable for each of us.

There are many forms of prayer that can help us connect with our sense of the divine power in the universe. We can say traditional prayers learned from our religious upbringing, or we can create our own form of casually conversing with God, the all-being universal consciousness.

I have found it strengthening to shift from prayer that pleads for help to prayer that expresses gratitude for help that is already on its way. Instead of saying "Please help me with this...," I might say — "Thank you, God, for guiding me through this challenge. I feel your presence." That way I have the comfort of divine assistance immediately upon uttering the prayer. Also, pleading prayer that focuses on lack is echoing that scarcity and reinforcing it. And when I am praying for something specific, I always ask God to provide it only "if it is in the highest good for all concerned."

Whatever way we choose to pray, the act of engaging in prayer helps us connect with a beneficent higher power and surrender to the invisible universe beyond our control. Prayer widens our perspective, expanding our consciousness from myopic focus on our own little stories to the "big picture" where unseen forces are at play.

In addition to these types of prayer, there is also the practice of repeating a short phrase or mantra to connect with spirit and raise consciousness. In all languages, the single syllable "Om" or "Aum" is the universal sound of peace or the name of God. There are innumerable Sanskrit mantras that call upon the various forms of God and the divine mother — chants that honor Shiva and Shakti energy and evoke the blessings of God.

The repetition of mantra is beneficial in any language. It is both a way of calling upon God and a way of calling for goodness in life. A simple, yet powerful way to engage in mantra is to create our own mantras in English such as "Be still and know that I am

God." Mantras do not necessarily have to refer to deities but can allude to whatever we choose to manifest in our lives.

Actually, a mantra can be any affirmation or positive thought that we choose to repeat over and over again to strengthen ourselves and uplift our consciousness. Examples are: "I let go and trust life; God always provides for me; I am filled with love and light; My peace is more important than this; All is well."

Just as it is important to stay conscious of each word while uttering the prayers on rosary beads, it is essential to repeat each mantra with feeling. Whatever form of prayer or mantra you may choose, it is vital for you to have your own way of connecting with a higher power and expressing your spirituality as often as possible.

Finding peace and purpose — living with grace

As we learn to reflect on our experiences using the ten principles as our guidelines, we can learn to accept all life experiences with grace and achieve a deep sense of the peace within. Then we can carry this light-hearted, good-natured quality to all we do, removing obstacles and excelling at expressing ourselves.

Applying self-study, we can learn to be honest, open and receptive with people. We can pay attention to what we are thinking and feeling as we interact with and learn from them. This type of moment-to-moment engagement and reflective self-study can help us be the best we can be. It can help us become clear on how we can contribute more to others and fulfill our purpose for being. Part of self-study is asking to know what contributions we are to make and what services we are here to give to others.

Too often, many of us allow our Monkey Minds to keep us feeling separate much of the time. We need to get out of the habit of keeping ourselves isolated. We might seek like-minded people at church or neighborhood functions hosted at the library or community center. We can find events advertised in newspapers and online by searching the Internet, where we can access educational articles and seminars such as Oprah's Eckhart Tolle series. Or, we can join the type of groups mentioned earlier and work with others to contribute to the well-being of our society and environment.

Rather than hiding out in our own little corners, we can expand to reach out to others. We can begin to open our hearts more to feel a connection with others and start to appreciate the oneness of all beings in the universe. As we reflect on our usual pastimes, we can decide to spend our free time in positive ways with people who have high values rather than dissipate our leisure time with people who drag us down and encourage bad habits.

Through enriching reading and activities and heart-felt prayer and mantra, we can become clearer in each moment about who we are and what we have to contribute. With ongoing self-study, we can become life-long learners, always expanding in consciousness, discovering and pursuing our life's purpose.

Ongoing self-study offers tremendous rewards. Our lives become enhanced as we meet more people who are interesting, read great books that change our thinking and attend gatherings that broaden our perspectives. Our lives become an adventure in raising our consciousness and expanding our horizons. For developing beings, self-study is our life-long quest to keep learning, growing and contributing the best we have to give.

Look in the mirror and ask "How am I doing?"

As self-reflective, developing beings, it is helpful to frequently ask ourselves "How am I doing?" The Earth School classes and corridors are filled with mirrors. Every encounter with people, everything that happens, reflects something back to us about ourselves. It's our job to become increasingly aware of the messages and more open to receiving them.

When someone becomes annoyed at something we have said, it is best not to just dismiss them. We might mentally inquire into what may have offended them. Of course, we probably think that what we said was fine, but perhaps we could have delivered the communication in a way that they would have received better.

Maybe there was negative energy we projected without realizing it. And, maybe their response had nothing to do with us.

We all have those moments when we wish we could simply revise what just happened and be granted a "do over." Without magnifying anything out of its proper perspective, it is good to learn from what we see being reflected back at us. Just observe your effect on the people around you. When something seems unharmonious, simply recognize it. Say "Good notice!" and see if you can shift things for the better.

For example, I recall when I was in a store with a long check-out line that did not seem to be moving. I was late for an appointment and started to mentally berate the girl at the register, thinking she must be the slowest check-out person on the planet. My mind rattled on as I wondered what her problem might be.

Then, as I listened to myself complain, I realized that I was being unkind and shifted to being patient and friendly. By the time the tired clerk totaled my merchandise, I had shifted to honoring her and softly asked, "Has it been a very busy day?" She replied that she was working a second shift because another employee had called in sick. I was really glad that I had made this quick shift before I got to the front of the line. This time my own thoughts had mirrored the need to shift.

Another time when I was leading a very wonderful and happy retreat group, a couple of guests in the back of my van were talking so loudly that I could not point out places of interest. I turned around and asked if I could have a little quiet. Suddenly, there was dead silence and then lasting silence.

Feeling the energy of the two ladies behind me plummet, I turned to the one I could see and asked if I had offended her. She immediately told me that her mother had always yelled at her to "Shh" and be quiet. My comment had prompted fear and a host of sad, hurt feelings. Once she acknowledged the association to her mother, she was able to let it go and participate joyously again.

Sometimes the feelings we evoke in others go deeper than what is happening in the moment. The point is that when we are attuned to the energy flow of harmony, we can feel when something is out of harmony and clear it up.

In the spirit of personal growth, we can remain open to viewing what the mirrors are reflecting back to us. When we see others who are not happy with us, we can be open to looking at their point of view, addressing where there might be validity in their perceptions and perhaps shifting our attitude or behavior. Yes, we can learn a lot from what the mirrors reflect to us, and very often they reveal our blind spots and unconscious projections.

We are all Earth School students who are capable of making mistakes, then acknowledging and correcting them. We must again beware of blame. There is a popular saying that when we point a finger at someone else, there are always three fingers pointing back at us.

Instead of resisting what is to be learned, we can continue practicing our "Good notice" policy and welcome whatever we need to shift without blaming ourselves or anyone else. This principle of self-study is about keeping an open mind regarding our experiences so that we can learn from them, integrate the teaching and fully excel at living our life purpose.

Practicing self-study, we can explore every facet of being human and anything that will help us understand ourselves. As we grow in awareness, we can learn to use our strengths to overcome our weaknesses. Through such self-study, we nurture the core essence within each one of us as the place we access higher consciousness and our connection with the divine oneness.

Everyday examples
Review the following examples of the need for greater self-study and discrimination. See if any of them might be similar to what you experience in your life.

▲ Feeling obligated to spend time with people who are negative
▲ Meaning to get to an uplifting gathering but somehow postponing it again

▲ Knowing what would be good for you but not doing it

▲ Getting adamant and fixed in your opinion of people and things

▲ Not taking time to reflect on how you are living your life

▲ Plodding on from day to day without really knowing your purpose

▲ Watching shows and reading literature with violent or decadent behavior

▲ Being too closed to shift to a new perspective

▲ Not being able to shake off someone whose constant complaining drains your energy

▲ Letting yourself get caught in the negativity instead of shifting to higher consciousness

▲ Never having time to still yourself and access inner guidance

"Monkey Mind" protests and reality checks
What is your Monkey Mind's automatic response to developing ongoing self-study? Ponder the objections below and see if any of them might apply to you —

Monkey Mind: *I like reading books and articles that help me grow, but at night it's so much easier just to turn on the television and get absorbed in it.*

Reality check: Reading vs. television — Reading or pursuing some worthwhile subject online rather than getting lost in the television is a way to practice both discipline and self-study. The best way to combat the magnetic attraction of the television is not to turn it on in the first place.

Take an honest look at how much time you spend watching television. Just for one week, count the number of hours you and your family members spend watching T.V. Once you become aware of the number of hours you spend riveted to the television, you may see the need to wean yourself away from it. One way is to only turn the television on when you know there is a favorite show to watch or a good movie, and then turn it off right afterwards.

The same mindfulness applies to monitoring the value your time in front of the computer screen. You might turn the computer on for a quick email check, then turn it off right away. Or you could actually use your computer to connect to your spiritual community. It is a great place to meet like-minded people and learn about spiritual practices and new trends of thought.

There are numerous educational websites you can find simply by doing a search on www.google.com, such as Abraham-Hicks and Oprah. You might also look up favorite authors and read their articles and book excerpts online. For those who learn better by listening, there are many workshops and books on CD and uplifting radio programs by Hay House and others.

You might enjoy reading at the computer or sitting back in an easy chair with a good book now and then. It might help to create a reading nook in your home, a place with good lighting where you can be cozy curling up with a book. You can enjoy a wide variety of magazines on everything from homemaking and entertainment to automotive and mechanical engineering.

You might choose to go to bed before you are sleepy. Prop yourself up on the pillows and enjoy reading or writing in a journal. Doing reflective journal writing and highlighting your daily insights and gratitudes is a great way to end or begin a day. You can summon the discipline to let go of television and engage in reading and writing that do more to enhance your aliveness. You can still chill out in front of the TV sometimes, but less often.

Monkey Mind: *At heart, I am a deeply devotional person. Yet, sometimes I go throughout the whole day — so busy juggling tasks — that I don't remember to feel my connection to Spirit until bedtime, when I lay my head on my pillow and pray.*

Reality check: Remembering to connect with a higher power during your daily activities — It is quite understandable to get swept up in the momentum of daily work and tasks. Hurrying from one task to the next without ever finishing all of the things on your list can be harrowing.

A practice I have found very rewarding is to use transitions from one task to another as an opportunity to be grateful for what I have accomplished. I take a moment to sit still, close my eyes and follow my breath to the stillness inside. These "drop-ins" are a way to connect with your inner wisdom repeatedly throughout the day. They help you let go of your egos concerns and access your higher consciousness.

Simply take transition breaks between tasks to close your eyes, focus on your breath and use your breathing to help you "drop-in" to that quiet place within where you connect with your core inner strength. You can call it your inner peace, your place of perfect being or the empty place inside where there are no lists. You can drop into the stillness and silence inside of you where you are one with divine energy and all is well. Then, after just a little while, you can turn to whatever is on your list to do next, feeling peaceful, calm and refreshed.

I invite you to consciously turn transitions between tasks into opportunities to express gratitude and feel connected to all that is. Take time to feel grateful for each part of your day. Acknowledge yourself for what you have accomplished. Use your breath to guide you into your sacred stillness and connect with your wholeness and inner being. You will find it calming and be able to get more accomplished from this place of ease and grace.

Another easy way to keep your spiritual connection alive during the day is to remember to say grace when you eat, whether alone or with others. Most people eat three times a day, so this would be connecting with divine spirit at least that many times. Just this simple practice of blessing your food connects you with a higher power in a moment of devotion and gratitude.

Monkey Mind: *I do have friends who are always complaining and being negative. I have listened to and put up with them for decades. You cannot expect me to just drop them now?!*

Reality check: Handling negative friends — No one is asking you to drop your negative friends. You are being asked to consciously choose the people you spend time with and to develop friendships that are uplifting for you.

There are many ways you can handle the friends who are always complaining. You might see if you can cut the complaining a little short by empathizing with them and saying something like — "I know that must have been horrible for you, but what is possible now? What would you like to have happen?" Raising these questions might shift the conversation from problems to solutions.

If you have whining friends that just want to spin their wheels in the mud by re-running negative incidents, feelings and perceptions, you might choose to see them less and perhaps screen calls. Sometimes it's okay to say that you have only a little time and need to hear the short version or the bottom line.

Your first duty is to honor and nurture yourself. Practicing compassion, you must find a way to be kind to yourself and be gracious to the chronic complainer. Engaging in truthfulness, you might talk to your friend in a compassionate way about shifting his or her energy to be more positive about life.

I find that when I want to encourage a shift in a person I am close to, I say to the person something like — "I love you, and I am having a bit of a hard time with...." You can fill in the blank. Be as compassionate and as truthful as you can, always remembering to honor the person. The idea is for you to value yourself and your time so that you choose to be with nurturing people rather than those who drain your energy.

No-fault reflection questions for thought, discussion or journal writing

Now let's turn to your personal life experience. Answering the following questions will give you a chance to study yourself in terms of the people you associate with as well as the educational activities and spiritual practices you engage in. Take a few moments to reflect on the following questions.

▲ How often do you reflect on your own behavior?

▲ Give examples of times you were able to review your own performance and adjust your way of being.

▲ Recall a time you attended a gathering that was emotionally, mentally or spiritually uplifting.

▲ Think of a time you radically changed your opinion after investigation and reflection.

▲ How might you further engage in enlightening study?

▲ Describe the last book or article you read that inspired you or gave you new insights. Tell what you learned about yourself.

▲ What people in your life help uplift your spirit and which ones tend to drag you down?

▲ What form of prayer or mantra do you engage in, and what effect does it have on you?

▲ What inspiring educational activities do you attend? How often?

▲ How well do you feel you know yourself? What do you trust and distrust about yourself?

▲ What is your purpose in life? How are you fulfilling that purpose?

Now practice the Four D's
to transform any disturbing thoughts

- Identify the situation that has an emotional "charge" on it
- **Distinguish** in detail what you are thinking and feeling about the upset. Experience it fully so you can let it go
- **Detach** from it. Shrink its importance. Gain distance from it
- **Dip** it in F-G-H — **Forgiveness**, **Gratitude**, and **Humor**
- **Design** a new picture with your desired outcome

Good notices list

Now that you have had a chance to study yourself, take a few moments to sit and be still. Once again, be grateful for any insights that came to you. Let go of any feelings that the discussion may have aroused. Be very gentle and non-judgmental with yourself and others. Acknowledge yourself for being open to the discoveries you made by saying *"Good notice!"* Make a brief (mental or written) *Good Notices List* of the things you are now planning to shift to raise your consciousness.

Potholes to avoid

▲ Avoid people who focus on negative energy

▲ Stay away from activities that dampen your spirit

▲ Don't get too busy to review your performance

▲ Never be too fixed to listen to another opinion

▲ Beware of thinking you already know it all and are an expert

▲ Take care not to get caught in the treadmill and let it run you

▲ Don't lose sight of how you affect others and they affect you

Tips to follow

▲ Remember to ask yourself — "How am I doing?"

▲ Be willing to shift your point of view and learn new lessons

▲ Attend gatherings that are educational and uplifting

▲ Stay with people who have good values and positive outlooks

▲ Read and study material that will expand your thinking

▲ Focus on discovering and fulfilling your purpose in life

▲ Take time to connect to your inner awareness and follow its wisdom

From now on — Let go and relax

Now relax and let go of any emotions the reflection questions may have aroused. Sit comfortably, close your eyes and begin to focus on observing your breath. Slow down your breath as you inhale deeply and exhale fully. Allow each in-breath to focus you on the present moment. With each out-breath, relax more deeply and empty your mind.

Think about what you realized as you mulled over the questions. What shifts would you like to bring about in your practice of self-study? Ask yourself what your intention is for increasing self-awareness and expanding your consciousness. How can you enrich your life with heightened self-study? What practices can you drop? What actions can you adopt?

Intention-setting and intention-achieved

Take a few moments to think about what you intend to do. Then form intentions for self-study and ongoing learning from now on. Take time to word your intentions to your liking and state them as if they are already happening now. One at a time, begin to visualize yourself actually living each new intention.

See yourself and others involved in these uplifting experiences. See and feel yourself living your intentions with a community of supportive people sharing new insight and inspiration. Feel yourself opening your heart, remembering to have frequent talks with God. See yourself overcoming your Monkey Mind's chatter by repeating your chosen mantra or affirmation. See yourself learning from valuable books and bright people with positive outlooks.

As you focus on the richness of self-study, you might think of yourself as a sacred chalice, filling yourself with only the best life has to offer. Feel that your chalice is full of divine blessings. Remain still and savor this moment.

If you have gained any insight into choosing experiences that will expand your consciousness, uplift your spirit and enrich your life, you are already practicing this principle of self-study. The benefits of being a life-long learner will bring you closer and closer to accessing your highest being and greatest joy and fully living your life purpose. Keep in mind the inspiring words of Rabbi Hillel — *"Study brings us wisdom, wisdom brings us life."*

Chapter Five

Surrender to a Higher Power

"Good morning,
This is God,
I will be handling
All of your
Problems today.
I will not need
Your help, so have
A miraculous day."

This memo from God promising us that we are being taken care of is wisdom shared by Wayne Dyer. [38] Imagine that a supreme being appeared before you and spoke these words of assurance to you. How would it feel to have a higher power appear — perhaps in the form of God the father, mother nature, the great spirit or an angel — and tell you that all of your problems will be handled today? It might help you surrender your ego's concerns and breathe a sigh of relief. Can you let go of trying to control life and trust that somehow the universe will always take care of you?

The question of belief in God is a delicate one. You are to be respected for your beliefs and disbeliefs, whatever they may be. Some of you may have a strong belief in God. Others may question the existence of God.

Nevertheless, you cannot deny that there are forces present in the universe that are more powerful than man. There are things that are beyond our knowing and our control. We can call this powerful energy many things: "the prime mover, the universal flow, nature, mother earth, the great spirit, the great mystery, God" or even "the force."

In the Yoga tradition, sages speak of God *"as the perfect being pervading all things, the life of the world, the inner impulse of which each one of us has a share."*[39] There is an "inner impulse" that connects and sustains each of us. Honoring whatever religious or atheistic beliefs people may have about God, we cannot deny that there is this "inner impulse" we all share. This connectedness is ever present, no matter how separate we may feel at times. We can expand our perceptions to recognize the all-pervading goodness that surrounds us and the natural flow of life that is beyond human control.

The sages' wisdom

The zenith of our ten ancient principles is the sages' call to surrender to a higher power. Here surrender means learning to trust the power that resides within us and throughout everything in the entire universe. It is dedicating our actions and will to the supreme being or "supreme beingness we all share" — the divine source inherent in all life. It is devotion to the inner light or pulse shared by every being.

The sages say that only after the mind, body and speech have been cleansed by discipline and self-understanding has been attained by reflective study, are we prepared to surrender our egos to a higher power. In doing so, we accept that there is a flow to what happens in life and a force that guides it. We feel a connectedness with all that is and understand that we are part of a giant universal life force. In offering whatever we do to the well-being of the whole, we understand that things will happen the way they are meant to. We let go of our ego's attachment to particular outcomes.

Practicing surrender, when things that we do not like happen, we trust that somehow everything is in divine order. When faced with things we do not know how to accomplish or do not understand how to solve, we do our best and surrender them to a higher power, asking for guidance.

This is not surrender in the sense of loss, but in the sense of letting go of our ego's desire to control outcomes and replacing it with a higher consciousness of trust in the powerful source of all existence. In surrendering, we do not lose any part of ourselves or take anything from anyone else. We are simply deferring control to the invisible powers orchestrating events behind the scenes.

Letting go of ego and focusing on presence, we merge and become one with the higher consciousness of the universe. Surrender is freeing. We are happiest when we align with what happens. It's as if we relax and say to the universe — Thy will *is* my will.

We can perform actions as a contribution to the well-being of others. Happy to be of service, we can let go of any illusion of control. There is no longer any separation, just oneness with the all-being life impulse we share.

To live in service to this higher power and to all mankind is the ultimate surrender of our ego's passionate striving to control outcomes. *The sages claim that by surrendering and accepting the flow of events, we can transcend the suffering of the human condition.* Rather than being fixed on obtaining particular results, they recommend performing actions for their own sake. Instead of attempting to make things happen, we can simply set plans in motion and intend that they work out.

Life is not about fulfilling our ego's desires, but about something much bigger — the harmony of the whole universe. This does not suggest that we deprive ourselves, but that we put personal needs in proper perspective within a larger context.

There is a flow to the way things happen in life. We can either surrender to that flow or resist and get caught up in our own disappointment and perhaps even dramatize challenging experiences into misery. Suffering stems from not accepting what is. Once we surrender and accept what happens, we can restore harmony to our being, our relationships and our surroundings. While we do not have control, we do have input.

Following this principle of surrender, we must develop trust that whatever happens is somehow for the highest good. Everyone has had the experience of watching a plan fail and having something better occur in its place. The best advice is to make plans, take steps to have them succeed and let go of the outcome.

Sages suggest that the reward for surrendering to a higher power can be a heightened awareness of the vast blessings of being alive and a joyous sense of oneness with all of life.

Surrendering with faith and trust can lead to a sublime union with God, your chosen deity or whatever you believe to be the divine source orchestrating the universe. Such surrender leads to supreme bliss.[40]

Surrendering is strength not defeat

Thus, the fifth and ultimate personal growth principle calls for us to surrender our ego to this higher power, however we might relate to it. The most common connotation of the word "surrender" is to concede defeat as in waving a white flag on a battlefield. No one wants to surrender and admit defeat in an argument, in a game of sports or on a battlefield. Such surrender seems negative and an admission of weakness or loss.

In contrast, there is a very positive form of surrender that is having the strength of faith to give up trying to control the way things turn out in life. For example, we all have planned to take trips and had the universe make it easy to get time off from work and find the perfect flights and hotels. At other times, we want to go somewhere and the universe seems to keep blocking the path of travel with unavailability.

Once I was trying to get award flights to and from Hawaii for a writing conference and was told that they were unavailable each time I searched online for a matter of weeks, no matter how I adjusted the dates. Then it came to me that I was "pushing the river" and perhaps this conference that I was intent on attending was not right for me at this time. Sometimes when your path is blocked, it is because you are being guided in another direction. We simply plant seeds, create intentions, do our best job and surrender to a higher power.

The truth is that we have no control beyond that. *The only thing we can control in life is our own Monkey Mind's reaction to what happens in our lives.* Life's outcomes are not in our hands so we might as well give up the illusion of control. What we are surrendering is our ego's attachment to having things work out our way.

There is a need to surrender childish obsession with "I, Me, and My." We create our own suffering by taking things personally and dwelling on our little story. Surrender entails knowing that there is a huge interplay of myriad forces we cannot see or understand that affect the way things occur. Surrendering means having trust in the big picture and believing that whatever happens somehow contributes to the highest good.

Everyday examples

Here are several everyday examples of the need to let go of trying to control life and surrender outcomes to a higher power. Which ones do you relate to?

▲ Getting upset if others don't agree

▲ Feeling broken-hearted if your plans fail

▲ Making everyone else do it your way

▲ Becoming distressed if your expectations are not met

▲ Repeatedly pushing for something that's not happening

▲ Blaming yourself or others when you don't get results

▲ Insisting on taking action when logistics are not falling into place

▲ Rerunning thoughts of "If only I would have..."

▲ Feeling personally responsible for everything that goes wrong

▲ Being more focused on profit than on contributing

▲ Forgetting that you are not orchestrating the bigger picture

"Monkey Mind" protests and reality checks
What is your Monkey Mind thinking right now about surrendering to a higher power? What is it saying about relinquishing outcomes to an all-being consciousness? Take a moment to ponder the opinions passing through your mind. Read the remarks below and see if you can relate to any of them —

Monkey Mind: *You say to surrender to a* higher power. *I am not sure if there is a God or not. How can you expect me to surrender to something I don't even know exists?!*

Reality check: Questioning if a higher power exists — The question of belief in God is a personal one. If you are questioning, that is okay. If you are reluctant to believe that there is a God because you see so many "negative" things happening on earth, that is also your prerogative.

You are to be respected for your beliefs, whatever they may be. Whether you have a strong belief in God or question the existence of any divine being, you cannot deny that there are underlying forces present in the universe that are more powerful than man.

A belief in God or a higher power is intertwined with faith and trust. No one can explain why horrible things happen to good people. In enlightened thinking, there is a disappearance of the dualities of calling this "good" and that "bad." Everything that happens is just *what is.* People add the judgments about what occurs and then call some events atrocities and others miracles. Both are neither. They are just events that people categorize and use to make sense of a world orchestrated by unseen forces.

As I mentioned in the introduction, you can call this unseen source of energy by whatever name you like, such as: "God, great spirit, great mystery, source, nature, mother earth, the universal flow, the prime mover" or even "the force." Whatever you call it, this pulse of the universe links all living beings and permeates all that exists. You can recognize that this pulse-energy is present in all that is. You can acknowledge that there are forces beyond your understanding without needing to have a name for them.

Just know that you are not in control. Realize the bigness of the universe and the small role you play in it. If you look up at the vastness of the stars and contemplate the solar system, you will immediately see how large the universe is in relation to the little things going on in your life. Even smaller than a star in the universe, each person is like a grain of sand on a vast beach.

Monkey Mind: *If you are working on a project, how can you not want to oversee events and control the outcomes? To say that you are surrendering the outcomes sounds slack to me, as if you are not striving for excellent results.*

Reality check: Surrendering and still striving for excellent results — Surrendering the outcome does not mean slackening your efforts to achieve excellence. It simply means that you will do your best work to monitor your project to completion and not be attached to having it turn out exactly as you had originally intended. You understand that there are always forces at play that you cannot control.

For example, I set a schedule for my retreats. I always do my best to fill them. Sometimes a retreat just does not get enough people signing up for it. I have learned not to force the events that do not seem to be happening in the scheme of life. I simply acknowledge that this one particular retreat is not happening and allow that to be just fine.

I trust that my business will attract clients in other ways. One month when the regular retreat was cancelled, I was hired by a professional chiropractic organization to lead a full-day excursion for eighty-five chiropractors that was tremendously rewarding and much more profitable than any retreat.

When I do lead retreats, I give my 100% best. Each one is different in terms of participants' abilities, belief systems, interactions and degree of transformation. I facilitate toward the goal of transformation and know that the outcomes are due to a combination of forces, some within and some beyond my control. Sometimes I become aware of things I need to do differently as I learn from the mirror each client reflects back to me. As long as I have done my best to deliver a good retreat, I accept however it turns out and am grateful for the rewards and lessons.

Following this last principle, you have to surrender attachment to results, maintain a powerful intention to succeed in your projects and strive for a high degree of excellence. Then simply accept what happens, reflect upon it and see what insights or "Good Notices" come.

Monkey Mind: *How do you expect me not to have my mind preoccupied with thoughts of "I, ME, MY?" After all, I am the one doing the work. The person who is in charge of the job is ME, and having it all turn out well is MY responsibility.*

Reality check: Surrendering obsession with "I, ME, MY" — Yes, when you are in charge of a project, you are the one who is held to task for the quality of performance. However, the more self-absorbed and wrapped up you are in your desired outcome, the less open you will be to see the big picture and monitor the many factors at play. Yes, you employ your best efforts, set intentions and facilitate, but you must know that you are not the prime mover.

There are many influences affecting people, practices and events that you do not control. When you focus less attention on yourself, your role and your performance, you are able to be more objective and clearly see the various elements at play. You are less myopically riveted to getting what you want and more present to facilitate and respond to the way things happen.

It is best not to have your whole "I, ME, MY" sense of self-esteem tied up in any of your projects. When I taught writing years ago, I told students that they should not get personally invested in each piece of writing and be defined by it. Sometimes a piece of writing may be wonderful, and at other times it might fall short of communicating smoothly. I used to tell them, "You are not your writing."

Similarly, while you are valued for the contributions you make, you are not to identify your self-worth with the success of any given project. Just as I told the students, "You are not your projects." Some of your projects will succeed better than others, just as do mine.

Monkey Mind: *If no one has control of anything and everything is left up to the "flow of the universe," why bother exerting yourself? Working hard to achieve the desired result sounds like a waste of time.*

Reality check: Working hard for desired results when the outcome is not in your control — Not having control over outcomes does not mean that you do not have a powerful effect on orchestrating them. Your actions do impact the success of your projects. The notion of surrendering means that you let go of needing the success to look a particular way. You are able to accept the results of your hard work even if things do not turn out exactly as you intended. You trust in the flow of events. Perhaps the results are slightly different but could be far better than you expected.

Always remember that the universe may have something better in store for you than you had planned. In my own experience, I have been disappointed over losing a bid on a perfect dream house, and then found something so much more attractive at a lesser price. I have also found that when great, "irreplaceable" employees have moved on, the universe has always sent me phenomenal people to help with my business.

You must know people who lamented losing their jobs or relationship partners and then went on to find those that were a better match for them. Do your part well and trust that whatever happens is ultimately for the best, even though it might not seem so to you at the time. Then you need to accept whatever the outcome is. As one of my teachers says, "I ask for it all and am happy with what I get."

You can refuse to accept the results and be in denial if you like, but that will only increase your suffering. Remember that the sages say that suffering comes from not accepting what is. Once you accept what is, then you can be the alchemist. You can reflect upon the benefits of the way it happened and turn it into gold. You might use the Four D's and other tools at hand to design the outcome you prefer.

Monkey Mind: *When I have a problem in my relationship or on my job, I have to figure out the best way to handle things. I have to do whatever I can to fix things. I cannot just let everything slide and surrender it all to a higher power.*

Reality check: Solving problems and surrendering to a higher power — Yes, it is your job to do your best to solve problems that arise in personal or work situations. Again, you do your best and then step back and leave the outcome alone.

For instance, when you apologize for something you did or neglected to do, you know that you are not able to control how the other person responds. The person you apologized to can forgive you instantly, remain angry, hide resentment, give you the silent treatment or completely dismiss you from his or her life. You know that the other person's behavior is not in your control, so you let go of being attached to needing a particular response. When you communicate with as much honesty, clarity and compassion as possible, then you can be satisfied that you have done your part. You know that you do not have power over the perceptions, responses and reactions of other people.

It is very freeing to approach challenging situations with integrity and the desire to achieve harmony without feeling you have to manipulate or dominate anyone's actions. You simply surrender the outcome and accept what happens. After you do your best to "fix things," you trust that whatever happens will ultimately be for the highest good. That is all you can do.

No-fault reflection questions for thought, discussion or journal writing

Once again it is time to reflect upon using this principle in your life. How can you focus on surrendering your ego's desire to control outcomes and begin developing greater trust in life? Think about these reflection questions, applying our discussion of surrender to specific circumstances in your life. Remember to refrain from blame or judgment and simply look for insights — the "Ah-ha's!" of Earth School.

▲ Think of a time you consciously surrendered your actions to a higher power. What happened?

▲ Recall an instance in which you forced a particular outcome that was just not happening. What was the result?

▲ In what ways do you surrender to forces beyond your control?

▲ In what ways do you hold back part of yourself from surrendering?

▲ Describe how and when you feel connected to a supreme source.

▲ When do you feel separation? What steps do you take to overcome it?

▲ In what ways could you contribute more to others and be of service?

▲ How does your ego sometimes get in your way?

▲ What aspects of your life do you have difficulty accepting and allowing?

▲ In what ways do you attempt to "push the river"?

▲ What is your opinion of the Hindu proverb — "Everything received is a gift from the universe presented with wisdom and is to be accepted with joy."

Now practice the Four D's to transform any disturbing thoughts

- Identify the situation that has an emotional "charge" on it

- **Distinguish** in detail what you are thinking and feeling about the upset. Experience it fully so you can let it go
- **Detach** from it. Shrink its importance. Gain distance from it
- **Dip** it in F-G-H — **Forgiveness**, **Gratitude**, and **Humor**
- **Design** a new picture with your desired outcome

Good notices list

Welcome whatever you noticed when you reviewed the reflection questions. Even if you now realize where your ego gets a little pushy, it is all worth seeing. Let go of any uneasiness or other feelings that you might be experiencing. Allow your body to become comfortable and remain still. Make a brief (mental or written) *Good Notices List* of the things you are planning to shift by surrendering your ego to a higher power.

Potholes to avoid

▲ Stop over-estimating your own importance

▲ Do not force things when they are not happening

▲ Don't forget to acknowledge the forces at play in life

▲ Refrain from insisting that things go your way

▲ Let go of thinking that a lack of results means personal failure

▲ Avoid constantly going down the same maze when there's no cheese

▲ Do not waste energy dwelling on disappointment or blame

Tips to follow

▲ Trust things to happen for the highest good

▲ Keep your heart open to be guided by a higher power

▲ Allow plans to unfold or not

▲ Surrender your ego's desire to reign

▲ Remember to look at the big picture

▲ Notice when an unwanted outcome turns out for "the better"

▲ Let life be the way it is

From now on — Let go and relax

Think about what you discovered as you pondered the questions. What shifts would you like to bring about as you learn to surrender your attachment to having things go your way? Remember, the only thing that is within your power to control is your response to whatever life brings.

Sit comfortably, close your eyes and allow your breath to take you to a place of deeper stillness inside. Take big belly breaths, inhaling new life force, and hold it in for a few seconds. Exhale fully, lifting your stomach muscles up into your rib cage, releasing all air and old thoughts. Hold your breath out for a few seconds. Slow down your breath in this way as you inhale deeply and exhale fully, holding your breath in and then out for just a brief moment. As you become more relaxed, return to breathing naturally.

Intention-setting and intention-achieved

Ask yourself what your intention is for staying in touch with the universal consciousness and being of service. How could you alter your way of being at work or at home or during quiet time with yourself? Think about the possibilities for shifting your energy from focusing myopically on your own personal concerns. Widen your perspective to see the big picture and feel connected to a higher life force.

Spend a few moments thinking about your intentions from now on. Take time to clearly state your intentions, one at a time. Begin to visualize yourself actually living your new intentions. See yourself surrendering more as you apply yourself wholeheartedly to your projects in life. Feel secure as you trust that things will work out for the best. See yourself smiling and feeling worthy to have the universe's abundance flow toward you.

Feel relaxed and confident, knowing that who you are and what you give is more than good enough. Enjoy the experience of joyously welcoming life as it unfolds. Feel part of the oneness of life and the divine energy pervading all things.

As this poem by author Alberto Villoldo suggests, know that you are an important part of the divine tapestry —

"Surrender
become one with Spirit
Aware of your sacred nature.
Know that you are woven into the
Intricate matrix of creation."[41]

Summary
Achieving Personal Well-Being

To summarize, the second five principles are:

▲ Keep it clean

▲ Cultivate contentment

▲ Develop discipline

▲ Study yourself

▲ Surrender your ego

Following these principles helps us to cultivate ongoing well being and access inner wisdom. They guide us to achieve personal fulfillment and higher consciousness.

In ancient times, Patanjali wrote about the body being the temple of the soul. According to the sages, following these five observances helps us refine our behavioral patterns, cleansing ourselves physically, psychologically and intellectually so that our bodies become fit to receive spiritual knowledge and access higher energy.

In following these five personal growth principles, we keep our bodies and environment clean. We steady our minds to remain content through life's ups and downs. We exert discipline to achieve our goals. We study and reflect upon what we are doing with our lives to heighten our consciousness. We do our best and surrender our egos to the highest good.

Living in this way, we learn to accept and overcome our human foibles so that we can access our inner strength and keep our spiritual essence thriving. We focus our attention on being all that we can be, not from a place of ego, but from a quest for excellence and a desire to become clear about our life purposes so that we can fulfill them valiantly.

· Part IV ·

Essential Earth School Wisdom

Enjoy Your Earth School Lessons

I am sharing these ancient principles as guide posts to help you happily succeed in Earth School. I encourage you to hold them as high standards of behavior that you aspire to achieve.

Always keep it light as if you are the star of your own soap opera, comically dealing with the latest drama life has thrown at you. Dip all of your apparent problems in chocolate sauce (forgiveness), whipped cream (gratitude) and chopped nuts (humor). If you like, you can even visualize dipping those difficult people in a vat of chocolate sauce (compassionately, of course) if it will lighten up the situation for you. Remember the goal is to feel good about yourself and others.

Use the Good-Notice-Shift and written reminders

The *Good-Notice-Shift* is one of the best tools you can employ to help keep yourself content. When you see what is needed and are grateful for the opportunity to shift, no energy is wasted on regretting or blaming or judging. You are simply moving forward toward achieving the contentment you want in your life.

I suggest that you write the ten principles inside the cover of a notebook and reflect daily on how well you are living them, noting without blame where you could live them more fully. Develop a regular practice of reviewing your life in terms of these principles. You might jot down the ten principles on an index card to keep on your refrigerator or your night table or your office desk. Use these ten gems to connect with your own highest wisdom.

No one lives these principles 100% of the time

Please be sure to lighten up about how you now set out to apply these principles in your life. I recall a European Yoga teacher telling me, "Posh! You cannot expect me or anyone else to live like this all of the time!"

I smiled and told her that no one is expected to live these principles 100% of the time, except perhaps the Dalai Lama or the Pope. The principles present standards that we choose to live by, and we live up to them as much as we can as often as we do.

We are all human beings in Earth School, managing our human strengths and weaknesses, striving to have our higher nature win out over our baser desires. And, as the frequently-quoted saying goes, "we do the best we can with the resources we have in each moment."

Know that a little is great!

Remember to take small steps and give yourself big applause. Heightening your awareness of these principles in daily life is intended to increase your well-being and joy. Following these codes can help you deal with the ups and downs that are part of being human.

As everyone knows, at times we may take two steps forward and three steps back. No one is asking you to become a saint over night or to become a saint at all, for that matter. The intention is to heighten your consciousness and have you begin to practice principles that are life-enhancing and life-affirming.

A LITTLE is great! If you are a little kinder, a little more truthful, a little more moderate, a little more respectful of boundaries and a little less possessive, you will succeed at practicing the social harmony principles and get along better in Earth School. If, after focusing on these codes, you become a little bit cleaner, a little more content, a little more disciplined, a little more reflective and a little more trusting in the flow of life — you will reap the benefits of practicing the personal growth principles.

Tell the whole truth and forgive all

No matter what the circumstances are, *do not ever blame yourself.* Remember that you always do the best you can. Like all of us, sometimes you are more flexibly resourceful and other times you are more stretched like a rubber band. When we allow ourselves to become overwhelmed with more than we can handle and are not treating ourselves with compassion, at such harrowing times we are likely to neglect treating others with compassion.

If you practice managing your energy, you can be alert to when you are becoming stressed, stop whatever you are doing and be kind to yourself. When unpleasant incidents occur, do tell the full truth about your role in whatever did not go well. Telling the truth is the way you can free up your energy.

When all is said and done, the person you have to answer to is YOU. You have to make it all okay with yourself to have peace of mind. You need to let go of blame, express forgiveness and experience joy. When you rigidly insist on being right and refuse to budge, you add suffering. It is much more beneficial to free yourself by telling the truth and looking for the lessons to be learned so that shifts can take place.

Be a self-cleaning oven

A metaphor worth repeating is that we are all "self-cleaning ovens." Just the way we set the oven dial to self-clean, we can learn to recognize when we have collected stuff we need to clear and do it ourselves.

Become a self-cleaning oven using the Four D's: Distinguish–Detach–Dip–Design. Fully experience how good you feel when you are clear, centered and in your power. Get to know this optimal you, this powerful you. Tune into your best self and bring it forth. Accept no less!

Remember that you are an evolving energy being

Remember that while you have a physical form called a body, you are an energy being. You are an energy flow that exudes vibrations and attracts similar vibrations. You know that sometimes you might feel powerfully glowing with energy and at other times you might feel absolutely drained and tired. Keep clearing away any negative thoughts, feelings, beliefs or judgments that dampen your aliveness.

Your life-long quest is to nurture and contribute your energy flow. Let the best YOU shine forth. Focus on what you are attracting. Keep doing what it takes to feel good about yourself and your life.

Cultivate contentment as if you are the gardener of your own mind, body and spirit. Weed out the negative. Develop boundaries to protect yourself from being preyed upon by others. Plant seeds of goodness in your life and cultivate them. Make sure you give yourself enough water, sunshine and nurturing.

Start with greater kindness to yourself

A good place to start is to practice greater kindness to yourself first and foremost. Remember that everything that has happened in your life was an opportunity for you to grow into the conscious person you now are. There is no need to have any regrets or remorse over what is done and gone. It helps to believe that everything that happens to us serves a good purpose, no matter how unappealing it may appear at first.

One of my teachers taught me that self-blame is the greatest injury of all. Have unconditional love for yourself, especially when things are not resonating the way you would like. Treat yourself with loving compassion. Then carry the same compassion and kindness to everyone you meet. Being kinder to others starts with being kinder to yourself.

Develop trust

Try noticing when your ego is ruling and consciously practice letting go of its desire to control. Surrender your ego's wants and desires. Replace your ego's dominance with a feeling of connectedness to your inner presence. Use your breath to help you access the peace within.

Remind yourself frequently that you are being taken care of each step of your journey. Steer your course lightly, using these ten life principles. Trust in a higher power to guide you.

Know that when you follow these consciousness-raising

principles, you are attracting greater good to yourself as well as contributing to the well-being of others. Practicing these codes will help you excel in Earth School.

Let's uplift our consciousness and contribute to the highest good of all

If we are all connected, if we are all really one, then why don't we make sure that our actions, our projects, our business deals, our thoughts — all focus on contributing to the highest good? I recently received a $20 gift certificate from a local spa giving 5% of its earnings to the Humane Society. What a great example of manifesting business and serving the highest good!

I agree with Eckhart Tolle that a "new earth" is emerging. We are on the brink of tearing down walls of separation and learning to prosper in community. Imagine what a harmonious place the earth will be when we uplift ourselves by upgrading our values with a focus on the highest good for all. By practicing these principles and sharing them with others, we can boost those around us as well as ourselves. By expanding our commitment to excellence and heightening our everyday performance, we can enjoy greater contentment — and even thrive — as we make our unique contribution to the good of all.

Let us all uplift ourselves, each other and the earth by expanding our consciousness and living true to these core codes.

• Footnotes •

1. The Indian prayer referred to appears below in Sanskrit and English. It is the chant that introduces the *Kena* and *Shvetashvatara Upanishads,* ancient Indian literature of esoteric knowledge.

   Saha navavatu
   Saha nau Bhunaktu
   Saha Viryam karavavahai
   Tejasvi navadhitam astu ma vidvishavahai
   Om Shanti Shanti Shanti

   May we both, readers and author, be nourished.
   May we both enjoy. May we both be energized.
   May there be no obstacles and discord between us.
   May peace prevail over any obstacles within,
   Any obstacles caused by other beings or universal forces.
   May any problems of actions, speech or thought be appeased.
   May we have peace in our hearts, peace in out lives and peace in our world.

2. The *Yoga Sutras* of Patanjali has been translated from the Sanskrit language by numerous Yoga masters and scholars around the world in a variety of languages. As translations differ widely, I include those that seem most suitable to modern life, most often citing translations of B. K. S. Iyengar, Nischala Joy Devi and Swami Satchidananda. While the translations and commentary quoted are theirs, the discussion containing interpretations and modern application of the principles are the author's own adaptations.

3. The ten principles are discussed in all translations of Patanjali's *Yoga Sutras,* in Book II, sutras 29-45.

4. Iyengar, B. K. S., *Light on the Yoga Sutras of Patanjali* (San Francisco: Harper Collins, 1993), p. 136

5. Feuerstein, *Encyclopedic Dictionary of Yoga* (London: Unwin Paperbacks, 1990), p.309.

6. Sources mentioned appear on reference list.

7. Iyengar, B. K. S., p. 116.

8. Tolle, Eckhart, *A New Earth: Awakening to Your Life's Purpose* (New York: Penguin Group, 2005), p. 182.

9. Shearer, Alistair, *The Yoga Sutras of Patanjali* (New York: Bell Tower, 1982), p. 90.

10. Devi, Nischala Joy. *The Secret Power of Yoga: A woman's Guide to the Heart and Spirit of the Yoga Sutras* (New York : Ramdom House, 2007), p. 177.

11. Devi, Nischala Joy, p. 178.

12. Iyengar, B. K. S., p. 141.

13. Braden, Gregg, *Beyond Zero Point: The Journey to Compassion* (Louisville, CO: Sounds True, Inc.), audiobook on CD.

14. Gandhi, Arun, *Legacy of Love* (El Sobrante, CA: North Bay Books, 2003),   p. 125.

15. The Dalai Lama, *In My Own Words: An Introduction to My Teachings and Philosophy* (Carlsbad: Hay House, Inc., 2008) excerpted from *The Light Connection*, Aug. 2008, p.14.

16. Desai, Amrit, *In the Presence of A Master* (Lenox: Kripalu Publications, 1992), p. 167.

17. Qutotations excerpted from www.bemorecreative.com

18. Iyengar, B. K. S., p. 142.

19. Iyengar, B. K. S., p. 52.

20. Iyengar, B. K. S., pp.57-58.

21. Dass, Baba Hari, *Fire Without Fuel: The Aphorisms of Baba Hari Dass* (Santa Cruz, CA: Sri Rama Publishing, 1986), p. 90.

22. Iyengar, B. K. S., p. 142.

23. Satchidananda, Swami, *The Yoga Sutras of Patanjali: Translation and Commentary* (Buckingham, VA: Integral Yoga Publications, 1990), p.133.

24. Iyengar, B. K. S., pp. 152-153.

25. Iyengar, B. K. S., p. 143.

26. Desikachar, T. V. K., p.67.

27. Iyengar, B. K. S., p. 144.

28. Yogananda, Paramahansa, Where There is Light (Los Angelos, CA: Self-Realization Fellowship Publications, 1988), pp. 80-81.

29. Iyengar, B. K. S., p. 136.

30. Devi, Nischala Joy, p. 205.

31. Satchidananda, Swami, p. 145.

32. Iyengar, B. K. S., p.145.

33. Satchidananda, Swami, p. 146.

34. Satchidananda, Swami, p. 146.

35. Iyengar, B. K. S., p. 147.

36. Desikachar, T. V. K., p.70.

37. Iyengar, B. K. S., p. 149.

38. Dyer, Wayne. *The Power of Intention: Learning to Co-create Your World Your Way.* (Carlsbad, CA: Hay House Inc., 2004), p. 88.

39. Wood, Ernest. *Great Systems of Yoga* (Baltimore, MD: Penguin Books, Ltd., 1962), p. 26.

40. Satchidananda, Swami, pp. 149-151.

41. Villoldo, Alberto. *Yoga, Power, and Spirit: Patanjali the Shaman* (Carlsbad, CA: Hay House, Inc., 2007), p.69.

• References •

Aranya, Swami Hariharananda (1983). *Yoga Philosophy of Patanjali*. Albany, NY: State University of New York Press.

Bouanchaud, Bernard (1997). *The Essence of Yoga: Reflections on the Yoga Sutras of Patanjali*. Portland, Oregon: Rudra Press.

Braden, Gregg (2005). *Beyond Zero Point: The Journey to Compassion*. Louisville, CO: Sounds True, Inc., audiobook on CD.

Byrne, Rhonda (2006). *The Secret*. New York, NY: Atria Books.

Chopra, Deepak (1994). *The Seven Spiritual Laws of Success: A Practical Guide to the Fulfillment of Your Dreams*. San Rafael, CA: New World Library.

Chopra, Deepak (2003). *The Spontaneous Fulfillment of Desire: Harnessing the Infinite Power of Coincidence*. New York, NY: Harmony Books.

Dalai Lama (2008). *In My Own Words: An Introduction to My Teachings and Philosophy*. Carlsbad: Hay House, Inc., from *The Light Connection*, August 2008, p.14.

Dass, Baba Hari (1986). *Fire Without Fuel: The Aphorisms of Baba Hari Dass*. Santa Cruz, CA: Sri Rama Publishing.

Desai, Amrit (1992). *In The Presence of a Master—Gurudev Amrit Desai*. Lenox, MA: Kripalu Publications.

Desikachar, T. K. V (1987). *Reflections on Yoga Sutra-s of Patanjali*. Chennai, India: Krishnamacharya Yoga Mandiram.

Desikachar, T. K. V with Cravens, R. H. (1998). *Health, Healing and Beyond: Yoga & the Living Tradition of Krishnamacharya*. Ontario: Aperture Foundation, Inc.

Devi, Nischala Joy (2007). *The Secret Power of Yoga: A Woman's Guide to the Heart and Spirit of the Yoga Sutras*. New York, NY: Random House, Inc.

Dyer, Wayne (1988). How to Get What You Really, Really, Really, Really Want and Improve Your Life Using the Wisdom of the Ages, DVD. New York, NY: Winstar TV and Video.

Dyer, Wayne (2004). *The Power of Intention: Learning to Co-create Your World Your Way*. Carlsbad, CA: Hay House Inc.

Feuerstein, Georg (1989). *The Yoga-Sutra of Patanjali: A New Translation and Commentary*. Rochester, Vermont: Inner Traditions International.

Feuerstein, Georg (1990). *Encyclopedic Dictionary of Yoga*. London, England: Unwin Hyman Limited.

Gandhi, Arun (2003). *Legacy of Love: My Education in the Path of Nonviolence.* El Sobrante, CA: North Bay Books.

Hay, Louise L. (1984). *You Can Heal Your Life.* Carson, CA: Hay House.

Hicks, Esther and Jerry (2007). *Introducing Abraham: The Secret Behind the Secret.* Carlsbad, CA: Hay House DVD.

Hicks, Esther and Jerry (2007). *The Law of Attraction in Action: The Teachings of Abraham.* Carlsbad, CA: Hay House DVD.

Iyengar, B. K. S. (1993). *Light on the Yoga Sutras of Patanjali.* London, England: Harper Collins Publishers.

Miller, Barbara Stoler (1995). *Yoga Discipline of Freedom: The Yoga Sutra Attributed to Patanjali.* New York, NY: Random House, Inc.

Prabhavananda, Swami and Isherwood, Christopher (1981). *How to Know God: The Yoga Aphorisms of Patanjali.* Hollywood, CA: Vedanta Society of Southern California.

Satchidananda, Sri Swami (1990). *The Yoga Sutras of Patanjali: Translation and Commentary.* Buckingham, VA: Integral Yoga Publications.

Shearer, Alistair (1882). *The Yoga Sutras of Patanjali: Translated and Introduced by Alistair Shearer.* New York, NY: Random House.

Taimni, I. K. (1961). *The Science of Yoga: The Yoga Sutras of Patanjali.* Madras, India: The Theosophical Publishing House.

Tolle, Eckhart (2005). *A New Earth: Awakening to Your Life's Purpose.* New York, NY: Penguin Group.

Villoldo, Alberto (2007). *Yoga, Power, and Spirit: Patanjali the Shaman.* Carlsbad, CA: Hay House, Inc.

Wood, Ernest (1962). *Great Systems of Yoga.* Baltimore, MD: Penguin Books, Ltd.

Yogananda, Paramahansa (1988). *Where There is Light.* Los Angelos, CA: Self-Realization Fellowship Publications.

Also Available

YogaLife: 10 Steps to Freedom
A practical guide to living
the principles of Yoga
Create more peace in your life with a 47-page guide to living the Yoga principles designed for students and teachers of Yoga. Both book and two-CD set summarize the eight limbs of Yoga with Sanskrit names. They contain easy-to-understand explanations, reflection questions, meditations, inspirational quotations and affirmations for each of ten Yoga principles. The CD, in Johanna's voice, is set to a relaxing background of harp and flute music.

Perfect little gifts for the yogis in your life
YogaLife Pocketful of Principles
Carry the Yoga principles with you. This tiny illustrated minibook (2.75x3.25, 72 pp) has a definition, one reflection question, affirmation, Haiku poem and Sanskrit pronunciation for each Yoga principle (Yama and Niyama).

Yoga Principle Notecards and
101 Affirmations in a Tiny Tote
Choose a set of ten illustrated notecards with envelopes, bearing a haiku poem for each Yoga principle on the front and blank inside. Or select a tiny purple tote bag filled with 101 Affirmations based on living the Yoga principles. For example, *I trust my heart to guide me.*

To learn more about ordering **YogaLife** products,
visit www.yogalife.net/yogalife_store.html

Retreats and Workshops

Johanna is available for custom retreats and events,
workshops and speaking engagements.
To find out more about Yoga and hiking adventures in Sedona, AZ
Visit **www.yogalife.net** and click on the "retreat" tab.

· About the Author ·
Johanna Maheshvari Mosca, Ph.D.

Johanna is an accomplished writer, Yoga master and a teacher trainer. She has extensive background in education, human resource development and public speaking. All of her life's learning, accomplishments and skill are now geared to pursuing her passion – sharing the ten principles that will help everyone live in greater peace, harmony and integrity.

Johanna's first career consisted of twenty-five years as a high school English teacher, staff developer and graduate writing instructor. She earned a BA from Lehman College, an MA from Hunter College, a Professional Diploma in Educational Administration from Fordham University and a PhD from New York University.

Johanna's extensive Yoga education includes certification as a Kripalu Yoga Instructor and a Phoenix Rising Yoga Therapist, a 500-hour advanced diploma from the International Yoga College and two certificates from the Krishnamacharya Yoga School in India. Johanna is former President of the Arizona Yoga Association and author of *YogaLife: 10 Steps to Freedom* book, CD set and cards.

In 1992, after earning two licenses to serve as a NYC High School Principal, Johanna left the school system, moved to Sedona, AZ, and camped out for fourteen months. Pursuing her love of Yoga and Sedona's red rocks, in 1994 Johanna began offering *Sedona Spirit Yoga & Hiking Retreats*. Recently, Johanna's retreats were listed #1 of *"Ten Inspirational Retreats"* recommended in the May 2008 *Sunset Magazine*. Johanna currently enjoys writing, leading retreats and living in two wonderful places – Sedona, AZ and Oceanside, CA.

The Four D's

**Remember to practice the Four D's
to transform any disturbing thoughts**

- Identify the situation that has
  an emotional "charge" on it

- **Distinguish** in detail what you are
  thinking and feeling about the upset.
  Experience it fully so you can let it go

- **Detach** from it. Shrink its importance.
  Gain distance from it

- **Dip** it in F-G-H —
  Forgiveness, **Gratitude**, and **Humor**

- **Design** a new picture with your desired outcome

The Four D's and
Ten Principles in Action

Send us your success stories of how you
applied the Four D's and ten principles to
transform challenging situations in your life.
Let us know how you applied the principle(s)
and what you Distinguished,
how you Detached from it,
how you Dipped it in forgiveness,
gratitude and humor,
what you Designed and how it came to be.

Email: 4ds@cultivatecontentment.com

10 Ancient Principles

1. Practice compassion

2. Be truthful

3. Respect what belongs to others

4. Manage your energy

5. Let go of possessiveness

6. Keep it clean

7. Cultivate contentment

8. Develop discipline

9. Study yourself

10. Surrender to a higher power

Cultivate contentment as if you are the
gardener of your own mind, body and spirit.
Weed out the negative.
Develop boundaries to protect yourself
from being preyed upon by others.
Plant seeds of goodness in your life and cultivate them.
Make sure you give yourself
enough water, sunshine and nurturing.

May All Beings Be Happy ♥ Namaste

For details about *Cultivate Contentment*

CD set in the
author's voice,
and other
Cultivate
Contentment
materials,
visit our website:

www.cultivatecontentment.com